Sue Aiken and Robyn Wilson

CREATIVE TAPESTRY
MADE EASY

LITTLE HILLS PRESS

Acknowledgements

To our many students, past and present, we give our gratitude and thanks for their time and support. Particular thanks go to Pat James, Lydia Reynen, Marcia MacKay and Kristine Campagna, who helped us to complete some of the projects.

To our families, who suffered during the hours we agonised over writing, editing, designing and stitching, we also give our sincere thanks.

DMC materials used with permission.
© Sue Aiken and Robyn Wilson

Little Hills Press Pty Ltd
Regent House
37-43 Alexander Street
Crows Nest NSW 2065
Australia

Tavistock House
34 Bromham Road
Bedford MK40 2QD
United Kingdom

ISBN 1 86315 025 0

Cover by NB Design
Designed by IIC
Illustrations and photographs by the Authors.

Printed in Hong Kong

All rights reserved. No part of this publication may be reproduced, stored in a retrieval system, or transmitted in any form or by any means, electronic, mechanical, photocopying, recording or otherwise, without the prior permission in writing of the publishers.

CONTENTS

Introduction	**4**
1 Materials used in Creative Tapestry	**5**

Types of canvas
Threads available and how to use them
Needle types and sizes
Frames and setting up a working space

2 Getting Started	**15**

Lots of helpful hints
Answers to questions asked by students

3 The Stitches	**23**

Basic Creative Tapestry stitches shown
on single and double weave canvas
How to stitch them
Where to use them
Threads to use and effects they will create

4 Creative Tapestry Projects	**41**

Wooden Pin Cushion with Tapestry Top
Floral Bell Pull
Decor Doorstop
Novelty Clowns for children's rooms
Autumn Leaves Tapestry Clock
Mulit-textured Glasses Case

5 Finishing Techniques	**65**

Hints on framing completed designs
Assembling the Wooden Base Pin Cushion
Making up the Tapestry Bell Pull
Making up the Decor Doorstop
Framing a design in a Flexihoop
Assembling the Tapestry Clock
Making up the Glasses Case

Glossary	**78**
Suppliers	**79**
Index	**80**

INTRODUCTION

Creative Tapestry, as we know it today, is not something new. It is the revival of an old craft to which we can add all the new and exciting threads and canvases available in the modern world.

During our years as teachers with The Tapestry Guild, we have had the pleasure of coming into contact with many tapestry enthusiasts and students. Through our many classes, workshops and correspondence courses, and the setting up of many exhibitions, we have discovered that teaching is a two-way process. We have learnt so much about our craft from these years, and in this book we hope to share it with you.

This book is not based on any one of our courses, but rather aims to give a broad introduction to the world of Creative Tapestry.

We look at the equipment needed; the basic stitches, how to do them, where to use them, and what effects can be created with them; lots of different threads, with tricks and methods for their use; plus many helpful hints on how to achieve a professional look to your work.

We also present a variety of projects that will help you practise the techniques outlined. The projects have been included to give an idea of the great scope there is for Creative Tapestry work.

All of the stitching and thread techniques covered can also be applied to creative work using commercially pre-printed canvases. Photographs of a selection of these appear throughout the book, with descriptions of some of the threads and stitches that can be used to complete them.

A number of different ways of finishing creative projects, ready for use or display, are also discussed in detail. These give alternative ways to assemble your completed canvases.

We hope this book gives you many hours of enjoyment by opening up a whole new world of Creative Tapestry.

1
MATERIALS REQUIRED

Basic Creative Tapestry requirements are:
Canvas - the foundation on which to create
Threads - the mediums used to create
Needles - the means of applying the mediums.

Tapestry threads shown from left to right - Tapestry Wool, Soft Cotton, Stranded Cotton, Ribbon Floss, Medici Wool, Pearl 5 and Pearl 3 Cotton with samples of both Mono and Penelope Canvas.

CANVASES

There are three readily available types of tapestry canvas:

Regular Mono Canvas

It is a single weave canvas available in several gauges. This type of canvas is somewhat unstable because the intersections of the meshes are not secured, so they can slip and slide making it very hard to keep the stitching even. Regular Mono Canvas is often made of a slightly heavier thread than other canvases, and has a polished look due to the extra sizing used in manufacture. The purpose of the extra sizing is to try to keep the threads in place and separated while being woven and worked.

We do not really recommend using Regular Mono Canvas, and it is definitely not suitable for beginners. If you are doing designs with many eyelet stitches, it can be useful because the threads do come apart more easily, but generally the unstable nature of the weave makes it difficult to work with and so we tend to use Interlock Mono Canvas.

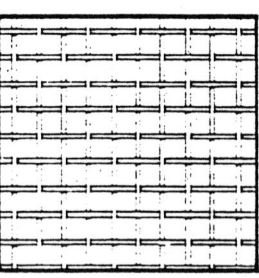

Regular Mono

Interlock Mono Canvas

Although another single weave canvas, Interlock Mono Canvas is made of a thinner thread than regular mono, and is more intricately woven. Unless you look very closely, it can appear to be the same as Regular Mono, but on close inspection you will see that Interlock Mono Canvas has the addition of a tiny thread wrapped around the mesh at the junction of the vertical and horizontal threads. Interlock canvas is sometimes referred to as Leno Canvas.

Because the intersections of the meshes are secured, interlock canvas is very stable, which makes it easier to keep a nice even tension to the stitching. Interlock Mono Canvas also has a very even mesh count in both directions, making it a good canvas to use for graph work.

We recommend Interlock Mono Canvas for Creative Tapestry projects that need to be worked on a single weave canvas. Interlock canvas usually comes in 100 cm (40 in) wide rolls and in several gauges, 40, 48, 56 and 70 threads to 10 cm (10, 12, 14 and 18 holes to the inch).

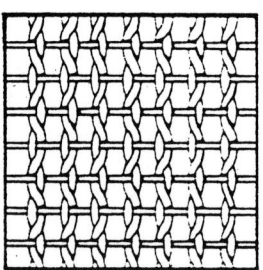

Interlock Mono

Penelope Canvas

A double weave canvas with pairs of threads running both vertically and horizontally. This canvas gives much more flexibility with the range of stitches and threads that can be used. Larger stitches can be worked over the double threads of canvas, and finer stitches over the single threads to give more defined details, smoother lines, etc.

Most pre-printed tapestry canvases are silk screened onto Penelope Canvas, usually using the antique (brown) colour and the standard gauge 39 threads to 10 cm (10 holes to the inch).

Penelope

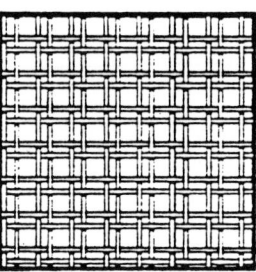

Canvas Colour

Both Mono and Penelope Canvas are usually available in either antique (brown) or white. As a general rule either colour will do equally well, as the threads should cover the canvas adequately. However, if using threads of predominantly light colours, white canvas is probably the best to buy; and if using mainly darker shades of threads, antique canvas will minimise any chances of the white canvas showing through the darker threads.

THREADS AVAILABLE FOR CREATIVE TAPESTRY WORK

Unfortunately, many people who work sewn tapestries still believe they should only use one type of thread to stitch the complete canvas, eg Tapestry Wool, Soft Cotton, etc. This, however, greatly restricts our creativity and, with the variety of wonderful threads now available for the needle-worker and tapestry enthusiast, we should be prepared to experiment with these new threads and textures, and turn our tapestries into realistic, three-dimensional works of sewn art.

Some of the most readily available threads are Tapestry Wool, Soft Cotton, Pearl 3 Cotton, Pearl 5 Cotton, Stranded Cotton and Fine Medici Wool. Totally different visual effects can be achieved by using these different threads, even when only the one stitch, such as Continental Stitch, is worked. Let us look at some of these threads in detail.

Tapestry Wool

Tapestry wool is the most commonly used thread in Australia for tapestry work, it comes in 8 m (8.5 yd) skeins in a wide range of colours. Some background colours are even available in 20 gr hanks (approximately 39 m [42.7 yd]).

Tapestry Wool is very durable and gives a thick, rich but also very bulky texture, so in Creative Tapestry work we usually use it only where we want to create a bulky, thick look, such as for a tree trunk, mountain range, ploughed ground, animals, thick tree foliage in a large tree, etc.

Because it is so durable, Tapestry Wool is the

8 Creative Tapestry Made Easy

perfect background thread for upholstered furniture, cushions, etc, and when worked in Basketweave Stitch it gives a very hard wearing surface to such items.

Until recently, if we wanted to work finer stitches, such as Petit Point, with wool, we had to split the Tapestry Wool. This was never very successful as the threads broke easily, but now Medici Fine Wool is available so there is no need to ply down Tapestry Wool unless only a very small amount is needed, say for a few compensating stitches around some area of fine detail.

Soft Embroidery Cotton (or Soft Cotton)

This cotton is a beautiful, non-divisible, soft, matt-finished thread which comes in 10 m (10.5 yd) skeins in a good colour range.

Soft Cotton is not as hard wearing as wool, but can be used as a substitute when a flatter, softer, matt texture is required, such as in the sky, the background to a floral design, for interior walls, flat ground, foliage between flowers in a garden, or hills on the horizon, etc. It is also suitable when a more washed-out, flatter, softer-toned effect is preferred, rather than a fuller, woolly look. Because it has a matt finish, Soft Cotton helps to recess parts of the design, eg the sky.

When Soft Cotton is first used, it takes a little

practice to get used to it, especially if you have only used wool before. It is necessary to use a looser tension with Soft Cotton so that it covers the canvas adequately. Do not to let the thread twist as you work. If it does it will not cover the canvas as well as it should. Drop the needle regularly and let the thread untwist itself before you continue stitching.

Pearl Cotton

Available in a number of thicknesses only two Pearl Cottons are used in Creative Tapestry.

Pearl 3 Cotton is the thicker of the two pearl threads used, and is equivalent in coverage to Soft Cotton. Therefore it can be used for any of the larger stitches where Tapestry Wool or Soft Cotton would be used.

Pearl 5 Cotton is the thinner thread and is equivalent in coverage to 6 strands of Stranded Cotton. It can be used for all of the finer stitches.

Pearl Cotton is a highly mercerised, twisted, non-divisible, lustrous cotton thread and is available in twisted skeins, with 15 m (16.5 yd) in each skein of Pearl 3, and 25 m (27 yd) in each skein of Pearl 5. Pearl 5 is also available in 48 m (52 yd) balls.

Pearl cottons can be used instead of other threads whenever a rich, thick, pearly lustre is required. This will help to make a feature of that part of the design. It has more shine than Stranded Cotton but less than

Soft Cotton wears easily, so it is best to use short lengths of no more than 30 cm (12 in), or you will find the thread breaking or wearing very thin as you stitch.

Soft Cotton can be used for all the larger stitches, or any stitch usually worked in Tapestry Wool or Pearl 3 Cotton.

Silk, and so gives a dimension between these other threads.

Pearl Cottons look very effective when used to highlight flowers or clothing, or when used for roofs, sunlight on water or in a sunset, moonlight, hair, etc.

Pearl threads do tend to wear easily as you work with them, so the use of shorter lengths is recommended. When you untwist the skein, cut through the whole skein at the knot, then cut these lengths in half again and you will have the correct working length of thread.

Pearl 3 Cotton can be used for larger stitches such as Continental, Vertical and Horizontal Long Stitches or decorative background stitches.

Pearl 5 Cotton is used for stitching finer stitches, such as Petit Point, Candlewicking or Canvas Cross Stitch.

Stranded Cotton (Embroidery Cotton, or Floss)

Probably the most versatile thread available.

Stranded Cotton comes in 8 m (8.5 yd) skeins in a very wide range of colours. It is made of six strands loosely twisted together, and is so versatile because it is *stranded*. This allows us to experiment with different numbers of strands; combining and blending strands of different colours; and even combining strands of Stranded Cotton with strands of other threads, such as Silk, Fine Wool, Blending Filaments, etc.

Stranded Cotton gives a flatter, slightly shiny but smooth texture to the work, and looks very effective when used for skin, clothing, flowers, leaves, walls of buildings, etc.

The *correct way* to use Stranded Cotton is to individually strand out each strand, then re-align the number of strands you are going to use. By separating and re-aligning the strands before you begin stitching, you will find you cover the canvas more evenly. Thread strands that lie next to each other will cover the canvas better than those that are twisted together.

When using an even number of strands of Stranded Cotton, it is often easier to cut the thread at twice the normal length, and strand out half the number of strands you wish to use. Then re-align the strands, thread your needle, double over the thread through the needle so that all ends equal, then knot the ends together. You now have the number of strands you want to work with, and because the ends are knotted together they are more likely to stay together as you stitch.

The number of strands to use for working particular stitches depends on the gauge of canvas you decide to use. Larger numbers of strands, such as 10-12, can be used for larger stitches on larger gauges of canvas, and less strands, 4-6, can be used on finer canvas for detailed stitching such as Petit Point.

DMC Medici Fine Wool

A very fine 2-ply wool which can be used as a replacement for Crewel Wool in tapestry work.

It comes in 25 m (27 yd) twisted hanks, and can be used on canvas by combining the number of strands of thread necessary to give the thickness needed to cover the canvas adequately. It is best used for all the finer creative stitches where Stranded Cotton or Pearl 5 could be used, but where a woolly effect is required, eg hair, beards, animals, fleece, etc.

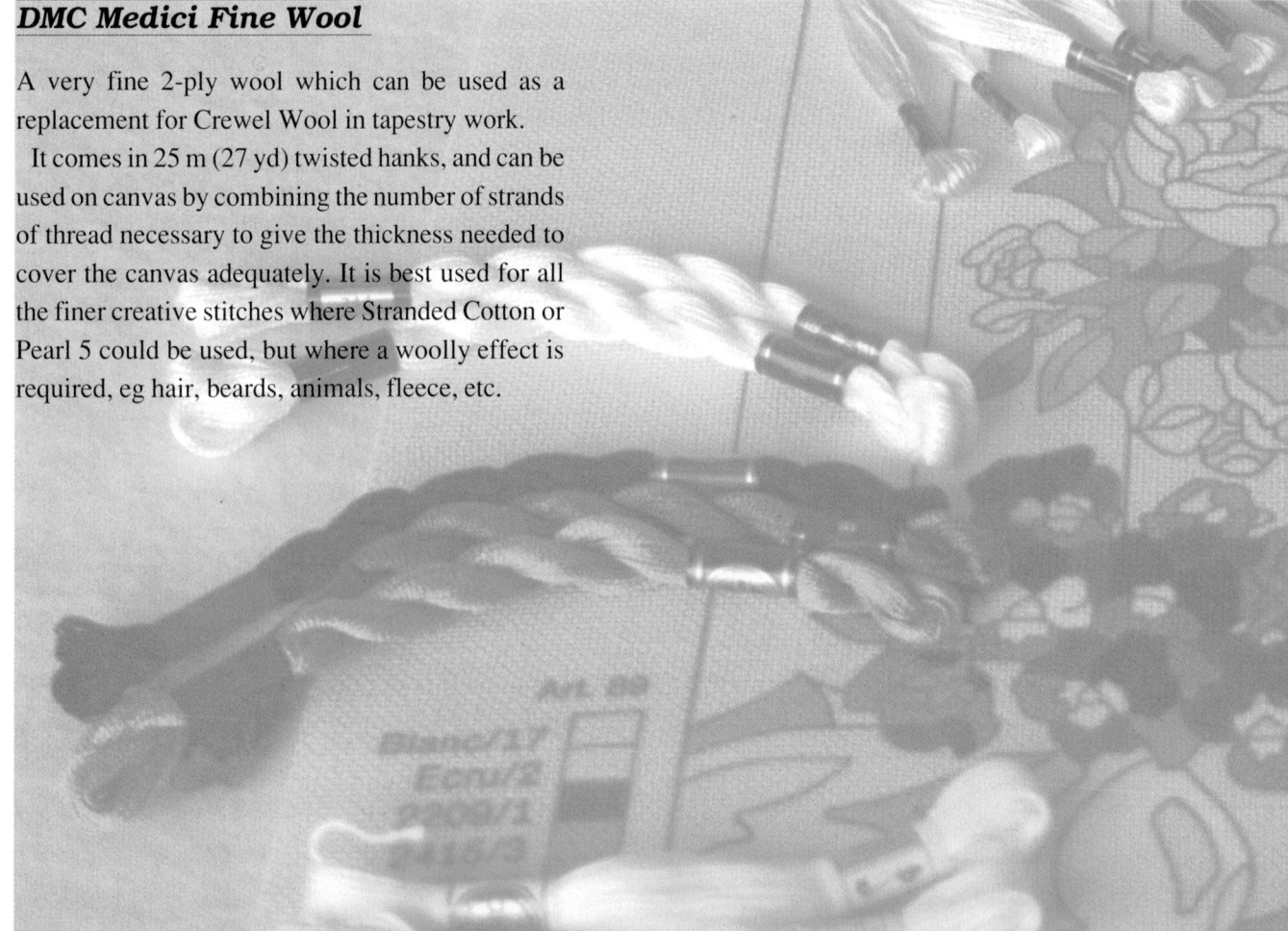

Ribbon Floss

100 per cent rayon mini-ribbon, it has the look of silk and can be used for tapestry, cross stitch, smocking and even in your overlocker. It is approximately 3 mm (1/4 in) wide, is colourfast, and comes on 33 m (36 yd) spools in a range of thirty-eight colours.

Metallic Ribbon Floss

It has all the properties of Ribbon Floss with the added advantage of a little sparkle.

Metallic Ribbon Floss comes in 37.5 m (30 yd) spools in seven colours - gold, silver, black, red, pink, blue, green, and an opal shade which is an opaque colour with multi-coloured glisten through it.

Metallic Floss does not stretch as easily as Ribbon

The secret of Ribbon Floss is that it is manufactured by braiding, so there are no hard edges as with ordinary ribbon. Its softness makes it pliable, less likely to twist, and easier to stitch. It stretches easily so can be used on many different sizes of canvas.

Floss, but it is advisable to use reasonably short lengths as it tends to unravel as you use it. As with other metallic threads, running it through bees wax helps to stop the unravelling, and makes it easier to manage and control.

The helpful hints given for Ribbon Floss also apply to Metallic Ribbon Floss.

Helpful Hints for using Ribbon Floss are:

1 When Ribbon Floss comes off the spool, it twists easily, so when cutting a length to use, run it through your fingers to get the twists out.

2 If you want the Ribbon Floss to lie flat and cover the canvas more fully, as you push the needle through the canvas use an extra needle, or your finger, to run the thread over to keep it flat and stop it from twisting or stretching.

TAPESTRY NEEDLES

There are a variety of sizes available in tapestry needles, which are blunt-ended so that the canvas is not pierced as you stitch. The correct size of the needle to work with depends on the size of the canvas you are working on and the thread being used. The most important thing to remember when choosing a needle is to ensure that it is not so large that it opens the hole in the canvas more than is necessary for the thread you are using. It is probably best to use the smallest needle that can easily be threaded with the medium you are using.

The following list will give you some idea of the sizes available and their uses.

No 18 Tapestry Needle - use for Tapestry Wool.

No 20 Tapestry Needle - use for Soft Cotton, Pearl 3 Cotton, 8-12 strands of Stranded Cotton.

No 22 Tapestry Needle - use for Pearl 5 Cotton, 4-6 strands of Stranded Cotton, Medici Fine Wool.

No 24-26 Tapestry Needle - use for work on very fine canvas or Petit Point work using 2-4 strands of thread.

EXTRA EQUIPMENT

Although we have looked at the basic equipment needed for Creative Tapestry work, there are some extra pieces of equipment which will make creative stitching easier, more comfortable and more enjoyable.

Tapestry Working Frames

A solid, well-made tapestry working frame onto which the canvas is attached is really essential to keep the canvas clean and rigid as it is worked. Frames come in a number of sizes, and one that fits the piece of canvas you have chosen, leaving about 2 cm (1 in) between the sides of the canvas and the side pieces of the frame, is probably the best to use. Most of us find we end up with a collection of frames in a variety of different sizes so we always have one the right size for the project we are about to begin.

A fully adjustable Floor Frame is the ultimate luxury, although most of our students now don't know how they worked without one. A Floor Frame, onto which the lap frame is attached, leaves your hands free, and makes stitching much easier and quicker as you can work with one hand above and one below the frame, passing the needle from one to the other through the canvas.

Scissors

You will need two pairs of scissors. A large pair for cutting canvas, and a smaller pair of sharp embroidery scissors for cutting threads. Make sure you do not cut canvas with your embroidery scissors as it does them no good at all.

A pair of scissors that has recently come onto the market is especially designed for unpicking any mistakes. It has specially curved blades which slip under the thread to be cut and lift and snip it from the canvas without cutting the canvas underneath. Although none of us like unpicking we all end up doing some, and these scissors, called "Lift and Snip", help make the job easier.

Thread organisers and thread files

New gadgets to help organise threads are constantly being marketed and which you decide to use, if any, depend on individual preferences.

Thread storage boxes help to keep threads clean and all in the one place. Some students find they have several boxes; one for each current project; and a couple of others to store their left-over threads.

There are a variety of thread files ranging from cardboard strips on which to attach pre-cut threads, to plastic key tabs held together with a split ring, and

decorative butterfly shapes, etc. The best idea is to experiment with a few different types and decide which one works the best for you. Some students simply use a collection of small resealable plastic bags, while others get carried away with several different organisers, each for a specific purpose.

A good light
Having a good light that shines directly onto your work, usually from over your shoulder or to the side of you, makes seeing what you are trying to stitch a lot easier. A light that includes a magnifying lens is the ultimate, but a standard light that you can angle to shine where you want it, is adequate.

You can also purchase a cheaper magnifying lens that hangs around your neck by a cord that you can adjust to suit yourself. A magnifying lens makes it easier to work areas of fine detail.

Setting up a special work space
We would all love to have a special room to ourselves where we could tapestry away to our hearts content, but very few of us have. You can however set up a special area of your own in the corner of your lounge or family room. All you need is a comfortable chair, a good light and a solid, floor frame that can be adjusted to the perfect angle and height for your chair.

Attach a length of ribbon to the handle of your embroidery scissors and hang them from one of the upright supports of the floor frame, then hang a thread file with some of your pre-cut threads from the other upright support. Place a small table next to your chair to hold other accessories such as a pincushion, glasses, spare threads, needle threader, notes and so forth. You then have your own working space, and when you have a few spare minutes to stitch, you don't have to waste time looking for your scissors and threads, or clearing a space to work. Instead, you switch on your light, sit down, and begin to create your own special project.

2

GETTING STARTED

LOTS OF HELPFUL HINTS

In this chapter we aim to give you all the "How to's" of Creative Tapestry. It is compiled from questions we have been asked by students over the years, and tells of all those little secrets which will give your work that professional look as well as solving any queries and allowing you to fully enjoy working Creative Tapestry projects and designs.

WHAT DO I DO FIRST?

The use of a rigid working frame is recommended for all tapestry work. It holds the canvas rigid making it easier to stab the canvas with the needle more accurately. It helps to keep the tension of your work even, and the project holds its shape better, requiring less blocking before framing. The use of a frame greatly reduces handling of the canvas which tends to weaken and soften it. Don't forget that the canvas is the foundation and a completed house is only as good as its foundation.

The first thing you should do then is sew the canvas onto a tapestry working frame.

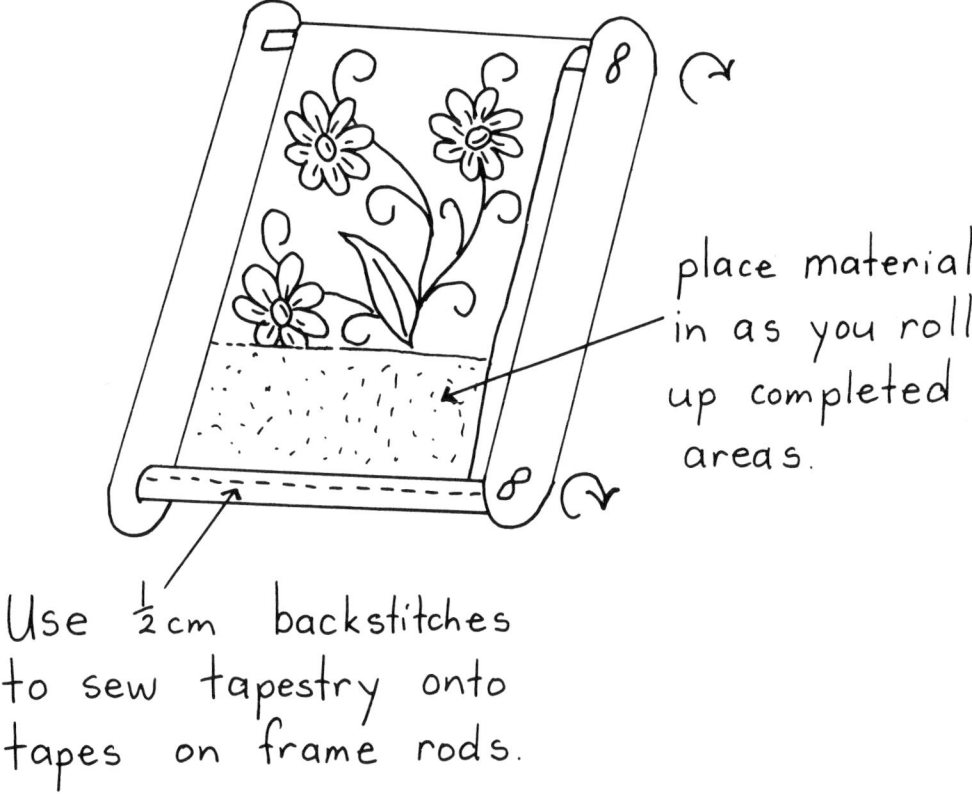

place material in as you roll up completed areas.

Use ½ cm backstitches to sew tapestry onto tapes on frame rods.

HOW DO I SEW THE CANVAS ONTO A FRAME?

It is important to sew the tapestry onto the frame correctly. Sew the canvas onto the tapes of the frame rods using 6mm (1/4 in) backstitches and scraps of Stranded Cotton . When sewing it on to the tapes, line the two rods up next to each other making sure the canvas is exactly even on both rods. Even being 6 mm (1/4 in) out of alignment makes a big difference.

The bottom of the tapestry should be sewn on so that it will roll up towards you, and your completed work will be covered, protecting it from soiling. Don't forget to place a piece of material in between the canvas and completed areas of stitching as you roll it, to stop the threads from rubbing against each other and the back of the canvas.

The top of the canvas is sewn on to the tapes on the frame rods so that it will roll away from you. This puts a slope on the canvas which will make it easier for you to stitch.

WHAT LENGTH SHOULD I CUT THE THREAD?

The correct working length for threads is 30-33 cm (12-14 in). Having the thread any longer will usually make it tangle easily, become thin quickly, and not cover the canvas correctly.

The use of longer threads also tires your arm very quickly as you pull it through the canvas with each stitch.

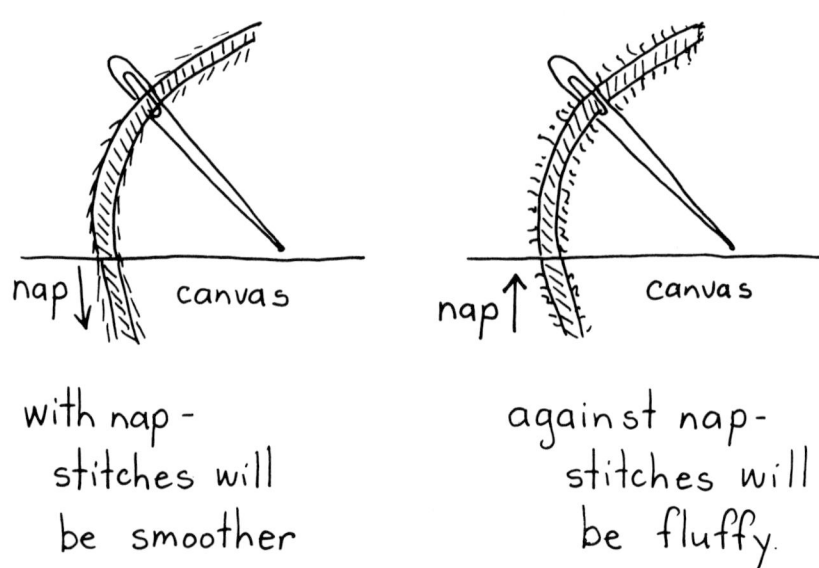

IS THERE A CORRECT WAY TO USE EACH TYPE OF THREAD?

Because threads are spun from fibres they all have a definite nap to them, similar to velvet. When rubbed with the nap the thread is smooth; when rubbed against the nap, the thread is rough. Stitches will have a smoother appearance when they are worked with the nap. To determine the direction of the nap, rub the thread through your fingertips. The thread feels smooth when rubbed with the nap. As a second check, you can hold the thread up and look to see which way the majority of the fibres are standing. Thread the needle with the end of the thread which will allow these fibres to lay flat.

Getting Started 17

HOW DO I THREAD THE NEEDLE?

Threading the needle is sometimes tricky. The easiest way is to first sharply fold about 2 cm (3/4 in) of the end of the thread around the needle. Slip the needle down and out but keep the fold sharply held between the tips of your finger and thumb. Now push the needle onto the thread.

If you are still finding threading your needle difficult there are a number of needle threaders available. For the thicker threads used in tapestry work you need a metal needle threader with two ends, one for the thicker threads and the other for thinner threads. These threaders are sometimes called Yarn Threaders.

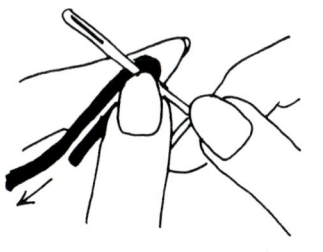
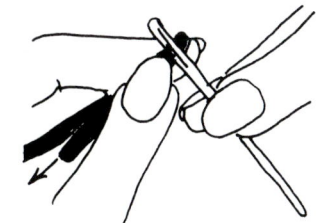

arrow shows direction of nap

HOW DO I BEGIN EACH NEW THREAD?

Once the needle is threaded, make a knot in the other end of the thread. This knot is to anchor the thread while the first few stitches are worked over it, but when you sew back to it, cut it off. Never leave knots in your work.

Push the needle down through the canvas from the top side (so the knot is sitting on the right side of the canvas), and bring it up again ten spaces to the right.

Begin stitching back over the end of the thread, towards the knot, and when it is reached, pull the knot up and carefully snip it off. The end of the thread is then securely fastened and you can continue stitching.

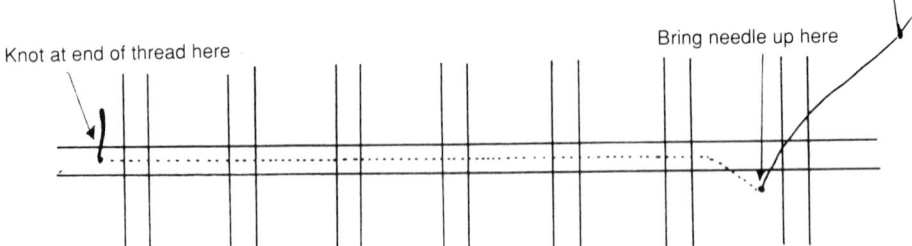

Although we often begin by using an anchoring knot it is not always necessary to do so. Once you have worked a section of the tapestry, you can join in the new thread by working into the back of existing stitches. The same rule applies as for ending off, always keep your work going in the same direction, eg Continental Stitch.

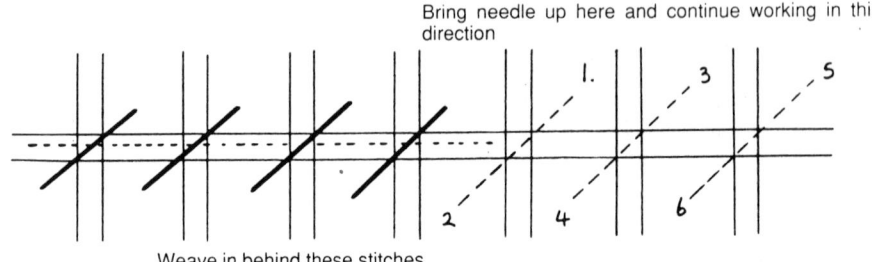

When you begin to use thinner and sometimes slippery threads such as silks, pearls and metallics, you will need to work an extra anchoring backstitch into the back of your work, and weave a new thread into the back of stitches already worked. This is especially important when weaving a thinner thread, eg Stranded Cotton, into the back of stitches worked in a thicker thread such as wool.

Always remember that you can begin a new thread with an anchoring knot as this helps to reduce thickness on the back of the work, especially when you are beginning and ending off many different types of thread.

Remember any bumps and lumps on the back of

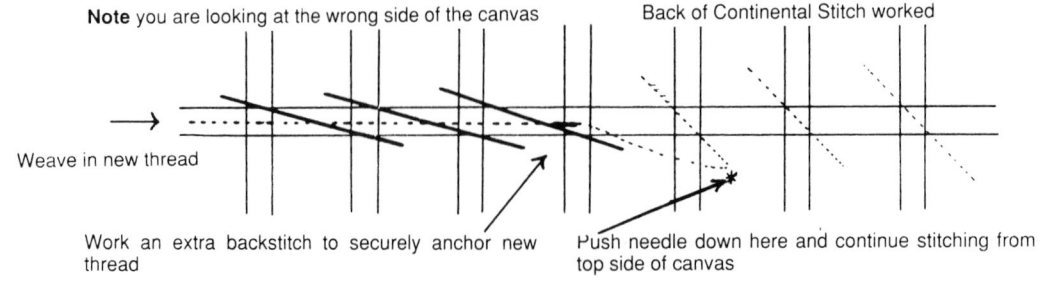

the work will be noticeable on the front when the work is stretched and padded before framing. Try not to weave too many ends into one area of the stitching.

HOW DO I END OFF THREADS?

When you run out of thread you need to securely end it off before starting a new one. Take the needle through to the back of the canvas and, working on the wrong side of the work, weave the needle through the back of at least 6 to 8 stitches. You should not, however, weave into the stitches you have just worked, as this will change the slope of the last stitch because you are changing direction.

Anchoring knots are particularly useful when you begin to use Pure Silk and metallic threads, as these can be very slippery to weave in successfully.

If you run out of thread mid-way along a row, weave into the back of the stitches in the row above or below the row you are stitching. Remember, however, to keep going in the same direction as you have been working.

If you run out of thread at the end of a row, weave the thread in upwards or downwards at right angles to the rows you have been stitching.

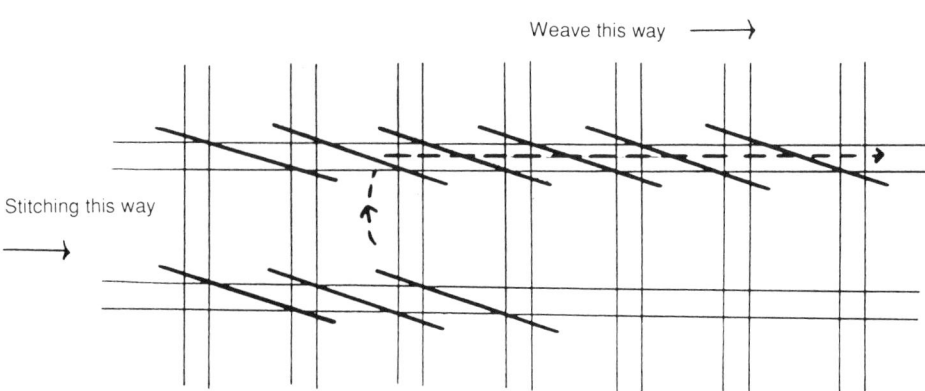

WHAT IS THE CORRECT WAY TO STITCH?

In tapestry work we always use the stab method of stitching. This method is worked by bringing the needle up from the wrong side, completely pulling the thread through the canvas, then taking the needle down from the right side, again completely pulling the thread through the canvas. Don't use a sewing motion (ie working each stitch in and out at the same time and then pulling the thread through), as this distorts your canvas and wears your thread.

WHAT DO I DO IF THE THREAD TWISTS AS I USE IT?

As you are stitching you will sometimes notice that the thread has become twisted. When this happens, let the needle drop and hang free, and gravity will untwist the thread for you. If you continue to work with twisted thread, the thread becomes thinner and will not cover the canvas as well as it should. It will also knot easily.

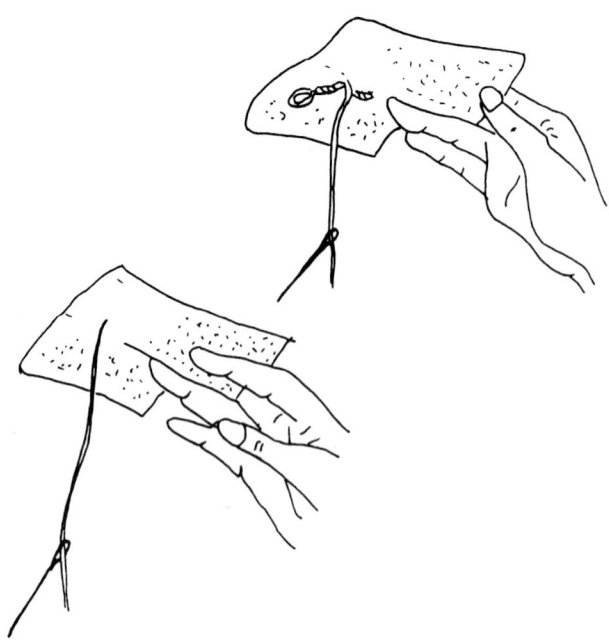

HOW DO I KEEP THE BACK OF THE WORK NEAT?

Many students worry about keeping the wrong side of their tapestries neat, and following are some hints that will help:

1 Trim off all loose ends on the back of the work or they will catch the thread you are using, causing loops and tangles.

2 Don't run too many ends through the same area as this will distort the surface of your work.

3 Don't end off very dark colours into the back of light coloured stitches. This may cause 'shading' on the right side.

4 Never use knots, except as anchoring knots which are cut off. Knots on the back of the work will show up as bumps on the front when the tapestry is blocked, mounted and framed.

5 When you are working areas of the same colour and wish to carry your thread from one area of colour to another of the same colour, it is best not to carry the thread any more than about 1cm to 2cm (1/2 in to 1 in) across the back of the work. If you wish to go a little further, weave the thread into the back of an area already stitched. If you carry long threads across the back of your work, there is the possibility that when the work is blocked before framing, these long threads could break and cause loose stitches on the front of the work.

HOW DO I CORRECT ANY MISTAKES?

Should you make a mistake of any kind, do not hesitate to undo it. You are putting a lot of work into your tapestry so it is a pity to spoil it by being lazy about making corrections when necessary.

If there are only two or three stitches out of place, unthread your needle and use it to unpick the stitches by pulling them out carefully, then continue stitching with the same thread. Do not try to unpick the stitches with your needle threaded, as this splits the thread and creates a tangle. If there is a large area to remove, cut the stitches very carefully with a pair of sharp pointed scissors or an unpicker, and discard the thread. Do not try to economise by pulling out large areas of stitching and re-using the thread. It will be kinked and worn, and will spoil the appearance of the finished work.

If you are using a thread doubled over, as with stranded threads, and you cannot unthread the needle, gently pull up the loop of the stitch from the top side of your canvas using an extra needle. When all the thread is pulled up so only the needle is under the canvas, make sure the needle is sitting straight up and then give a quick tug on the thread from the top side of the work. The eye of the needle should pop up through the canvas. If you need to unpick another stitch, turn your canvas over and repeat the above procedure to get your needle back to the other side of the canvas. Continue in this way until you have unpicked all the stitches you need to. If there are more than six stitches to undo, it is probably quicker to cut your needle off the thread, unpick the necessary stitches, end the thread off, and begin again with a new thread.

DO I WORK THE TAPESTRY FROM THE TOP DOWN, OR FROM THE BOTTOM UP?

There is no set rule as to how you work a tapestry. You work it the way you will enjoy working it.

If you work from the bottom up, you can roll up the completed area as you go, to protect it from soiling.

If you work from the top down, put a piece of material onto the wrong side of the canvas and roll it up as you roll the completed area. You can then put the rest of the material up and over the top roller, across your completed work, and pin it at the sides to protect the stitching.

One disadvantage of working from top to bottom is that it tires your arm and shoulder because you are stretching over the top of your frame.

The choice, however, is yours - whichever way is the most comfortable for you.

SHOULD I WORK EXTRA ROWS ON THE TAPESTRY?

If you intend to have the completed tapestry framed, it is necessary to work an extra two rows all around the edge of the tapestry. When framed, these extra rows will be under the rebate of the frame you choose to use. On some pre-printed canvases it is vital to add these extra rows or you may find you lose part of a leaf, or a leg. Or, you may have something on the edge of the design butting up against the frame, when it would have looked more pleasing to have a small area of background between the object and the frame.

Simply extend the colour you are using two extra stitches at the sides, top and bottom of the design as you stitch. Do not work the black border that is printed on some tapestries. Count this black line as one stitch and work an extra stitch, working both in the colour you are using next to the border.

If the black border is excessively dark, have some permanent correction fluid, such as Liquid Paper on hand, and 'paint' over the black line, so that when you stitch over it the line will not show through.

HOW DO I KNOW WHERE TO USE EACH COLOUR?

If you are not sure where each colour goes, before you begin stitching, spread out all the threads you have and place them on the tapestry where you think they should go. By the time you have them all sorted out it should become clearer to you. If you think you will forget where they go, cut a 5 cm (2 in) length and sew it onto the area where it is to go so that when you work this area you can match your thread to the colour you attached. Take out the 5 cm (2 inch) length as you work up to it.

3

THE STITCHES

In this chapter we are going to look at some of the basic Creative Tapestry stitches. These are the foundation stitches and you will use them over and over again in your creative projects.

We will show - how to work each stitch
what threads you can work it in
what needle size to use
and most importantly, where to use each stitch.

We suggest, as you read through this chapter, you try working samples of each stitch in the threads suggested so as to gain first hand experience of how each stitch is worked, and the various effects that can achieved with the use of different threads when working the same stitch.

Creative Tapestry involves 'painting' with our stitches and threads, and as an artist does, the Creative Tapestry enthusiast needs to experiment widely with all the stitches, threads and combinations of stitches and threads that are available.

To work samples of all the stitches in this chapter you will need to buy from your local craft shop:
20 cm of each of the Mono Interlock Canvas gauges - 70, 56 and 48 threads to 10cm (18, 14 and 12 holes to 1 in)
20 cm strip of Penelope (double weave) Canvas - 39 threads to 10 cm (10 holes to 1 in)
1 skein each of Tapestry Wool, Soft Embroidery Cotton, Stranded Cotton (Floss), Pearl 3 Cotton, Pearl 5 Cotton and Medici Fine Wool.

To work the samples, it is probably best to buy all the different threads in the same colour tone. Then you will be able to see the effects of the stitches in different threads, without being influenced by differences in colours. This should give a much better understanding of the effects you can 'create' or paint with your combinations of stitches and threads.

Basic Creative Stitches

MONO INTERLOCK CANVAS

VERTICAL AND HORIZONTAL LONG STITCH

The most basic of all the stitches on Mono Canvas is Long Stitch. These are straight stitches sewn over any number of canvas threads. To begin the second stitch you come up into the hole next to the one you started from, so that there is a long thread on the wrong side of the canvas as well as on the front.

Long Stitches can be worked over any number of canvas threads, but care must be taken not to pull them too tight so that they buckle the canvas underneath.

When working Long Stitches you need to use longer lengths of threads to avoid too many joins. Work slowly, pulling the thread gently to avoid twisting and knotting. Try to make sure that the thread lies as smoothly as possible to give the best looking coverage of the canvas.

Long Stitches can also be worked horizontally if that is the effect you require, eg for water, roads, paths, walls of some buildings, etc.

Before beginning to stitch the canvas, it is a good idea to decide which Long Stitches will need to be vertical and which need to be horizontal.

24 Creative Tapestry Made Easy

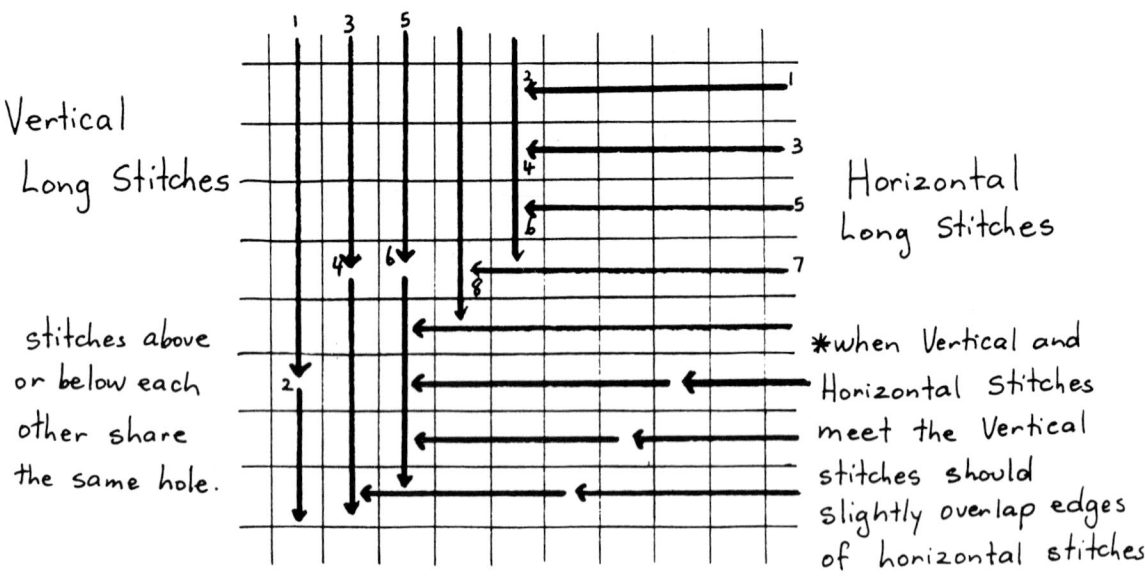

SPLIT LONG STITCHES

Often we find that using very long, Long Stitches does not give a very professional look to our work. One way of overcoming this is to use Split Long Stitches which cover the canvas better than Long Stitches, especially when worked over more than 7 or 8 canvas threads. Split Long Stitches can be worked either vertically or horizontally.

To work a Split Stitch, take the needle down through the canvas where you want the split to be, then bring the needle up again one stitch behind where you went down. When bringing up the needle you pierce the stitch just made, thus forming a split stitch. Try to pierce the thread as close as possible to the middle so as to get an even look to the split.

Split Long Stitches are probably best worked in threads that can be 'split' easily, eg Tapestry Wool, Soft Cotton, Stranded Cotton, etc, and the use of threads depends on the size of the canvas we choose to use. When using Stranded threads, extra care will have to be taken to make sure the strands do not twist but lie next to each other, and also that they are split evenly.

Split Long Stitches, however, can also be used to create some different visual effects in our work. For example, trees or bushes in the foreground of the work can have their long vertical stitches split fairly regularly to give them extra texture and interest, and bring them forward. When moving back in the picture the distance between the splits would be increased to add more dimension to the work.

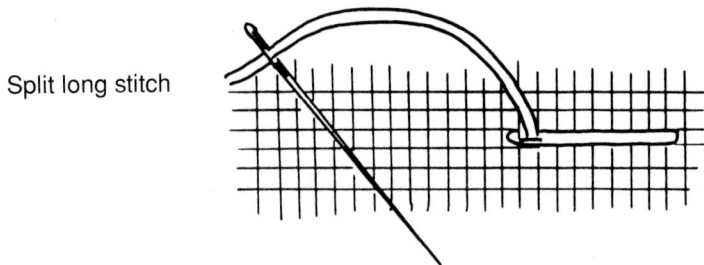

Split long stitch

The Stitches 25

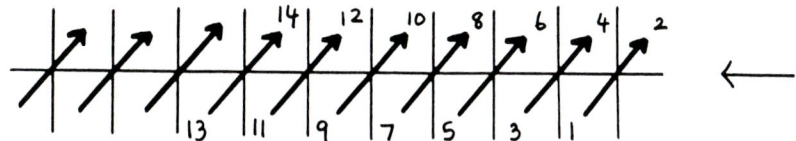

Down on even numbers

Up on odd numbers

CONTINENTAL STITCH

On Mono Canvas, the smallest stitch we can use is Continental Stitch, which is equivalent to Petit Point worked on Penelope Canvas.

Continental Stitch is worked the same way as on Penelope canvas; when working rows from right to left, work the stitches from bottom to top, and when working rows from left to right, work the stitches from top to bottom.

Sometimes you will have to experiment with the number of threads you need to use, as this will depend on your tension, and the size of the area to be worked in Continental Stitch.

The following are only suggestions of threads and numbers of strands to use as a starting point, you will have to experiment to find the correct thickness of thread for your individual tension.

On No 12 Count Mono use Tapestry Wool, Stranded Cotton (10-12 strands).
On No 14 Count Mono use Tapestry Wool, Soft Cotton, Stranded Cotton (8-10 strands), Pearl 3 Cotton, Ribbon Floss or Metallic Ribbon Floss.
On No 16/18 Count Mono Canvas use Stranded Cotton (4-6 strands), Medici Wool (2-4 strands), Ribbon Floss or Metallic Ribbon Floss.

Because it is the smallest stitch, Continental Stitch is used to show areas of fine detail.

Skin should always be worked with Stranded Cotton in Continental Stitch to give the most realistic look.

DOUBLE CROSS STITCH

On Mono Canvas, Double Cross Stitch is used for a very lacy and decorative effect. It is worked over two vertical and two horizontal threads.

Double Cross Stitch looks best worked in Stranded Cotton for a shiny, flat look; Pearl 5 Cotton for a fuller, pearly appearance; Medici wool for a woolly effect; or Ribbon Floss to represent a silky look.

The number of strands to use will depend on the grade of canvas, and how lacy you want the stitching to look. The more threads you use the fuller and less lacy will be the look.

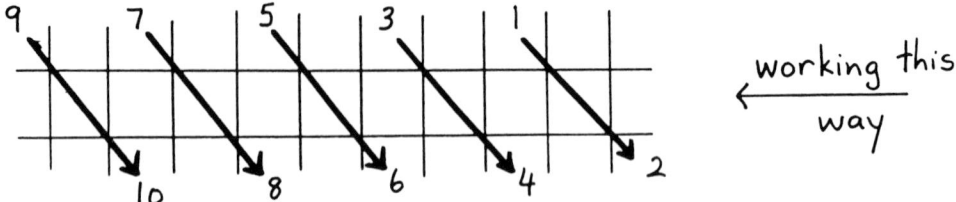

For Double Cross Stitch (Canvas Cross way), work the first row

Then work back over the same row

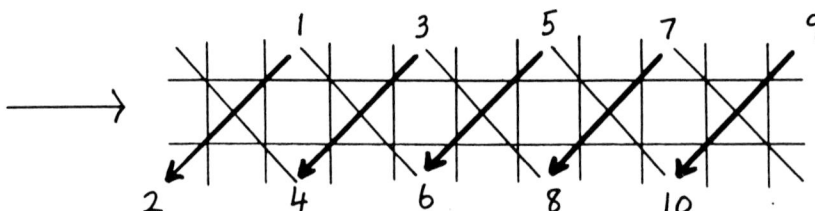

CANDLEWICKING KNOTS

Candlewicking Knots are one of the very basic Creative Tapestry stitches. They are just as effectively used on Mono as on Penelope (double weave) canvas, and can be adjusted to the look required by the choice of needle size and thread, including the number of strands of the thread you decide to use. For larger knots, use an 18 or 20 needle and one of your thicker threads, eg wool, Soft Cotton or Pearl 3. For smaller knots, use a size 22 or 24 needle and Medici Wool, Stranded Cotton or Pearl 5 Cotton. You can also work the Knots in Ribbon Floss or Metallic Ribbon Floss if a special and dramatic effect is desired.

Depending on the effect and texture you require, the knots can be spaced out, or massed closely together for a chunkier effect.

To make a Candlewicking Knot, bring the needle up through any hole and twist the thread in a figure 8 around the needle (this is where it differs from a French Knot). Then take the needle down through an adjacent hole making sure the knot is sitting on one strand of canvas. Tighten the thread around the needle and hold the thread taut as you push the needle through to the back of the canvas.

There are 2 important points to remember when working Candlewicking Knots:

1 Tighten the thread around the needle before pushing it through to the back of the canvas. If this is not done, the knots will be 'sloppy'.

2 Hold the needle at right angles to the canvas as you tighten the thread around the needle, otherwise the thread is tightened more on one side of the needle than the other, and when the needle is pushed through the knot will look uneven and seem to be 'loopy' on one side.

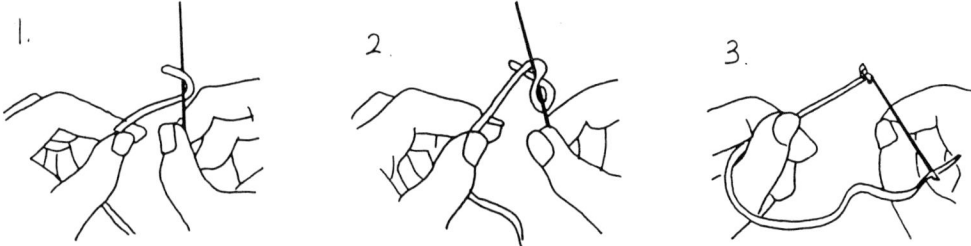

Candlewicking Knots

PENELOPE CANVAS

HALF CROSS STITCH

Although many people work complete tapestries in Half Cross Stitch, it is only used in Creative Tapestry when we want a *flat look* to our stitching and want to recess a particular feature. For example, Half Cross would be used for the inside of a building or tunnel, the area between two buildings, horizons, skylines, pathways, etc.

For Half Cross Stitch, the first row is worked from right to left, working the stitches from top to bottom squares along the row.

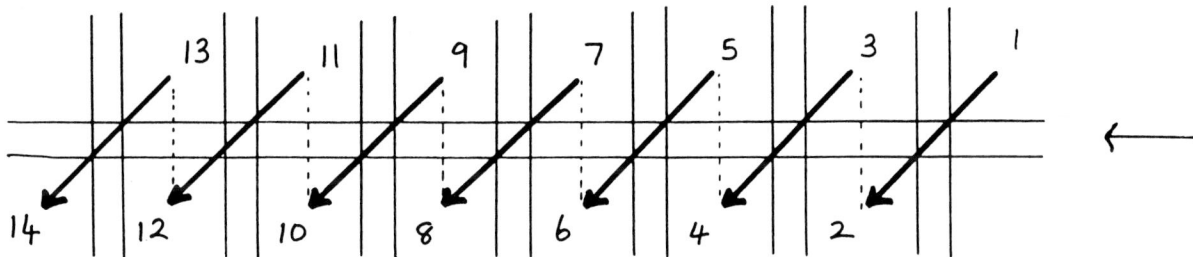

Work the second row from left to right, working the stitches from bottom to top squares along the row.

When you look at the back of the stitches you will notice that there is a *small straight up and down stitch*.

Half Cross Stitch is usually worked only in Tapestry Wool or Stranded Cotton, as the slightly thinner threads, such as Soft Cotton and Pearl 3 Cotton, do not cover the canvas as well when worked in Half Cross Stitch.

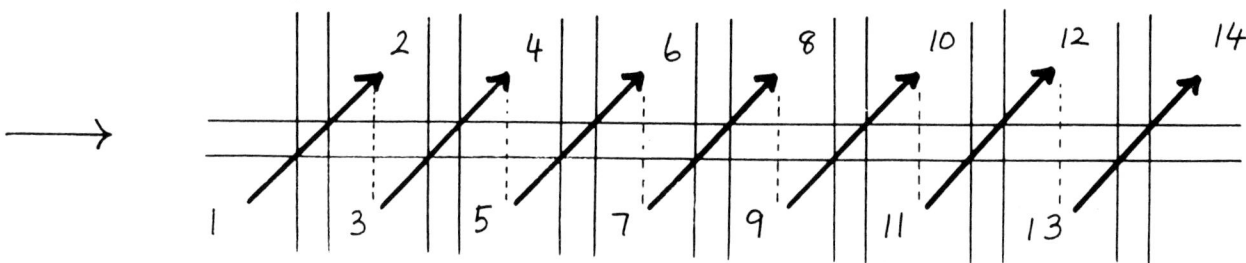

28 Creative Tapestry Made Easy

CONTINENTAL STITCH

On Penelope Canvas, Continental Stitch is the most used of all Creative Tapestry stitches. It is worth practising it until you feel confident, because it is the foundation stitch for many other stitches.

Continental stitch is worked in the same way on Penelope Canvas as it is on Mono canvas, except that on Penelope canvas it is worked over the double threads.

When you look at the back of the canvas you will notice that there is a slightly longer sloping stitch on the back than on the front. When you compare your samples of Continental Stitch and Half Cross Stitch, you will notice that although the two stitches look similar on the front, there are differences. The stitches have a slightly different slant, and the Half Cross sample is slightly flatter because it lacks the extra padding achieved on the back of the canvas when Continental Stitch is used.

These differences are even more pronounced on a completed Tapestry that has been blocked and padded before framing.

On standard Penelope Canvas (39 threads/10 cm), Continental Stitch can be worked in any of the thicker threads, such as Tapestry Wool when a woolly, thick effect in trees and foliage is required; Soft Cotton for a flatter, matt finish for a background or sky; Pearl 3 Cotton when a lustrous, pearly look is wanted for flowers, clothing, moonlight or water; Stranded Cotton (use 12 strands) for clothing, buildings or leaves; or Ribbon Floss for a special, silky look. These are only some suggestions but they should give you some idea of the different effects that can be achieved with combinations of stitches and threads.

Continental with Pearl 3, Canvas Cross Stitch, Metallic Dashes

Work the first row from right to left, working the stitches from bottom to top.

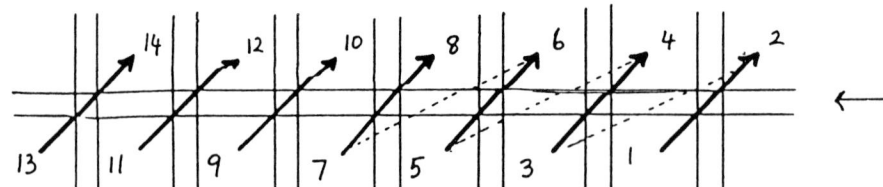

Work the second row from left to right, working the stitches from top to bottom.

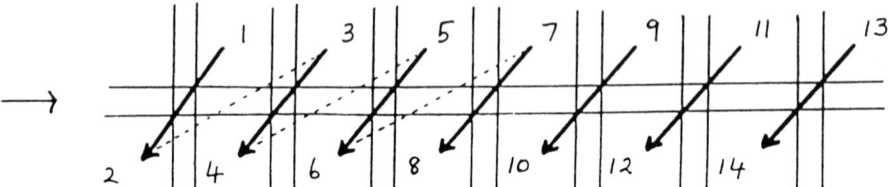

PETIT POINT STITCH

Petit Point is a miniature form of Continental Stitch and is the smallest stitch that can be worked on Penelope Canvas. When working Petit Point Stitch, we are actually breaking up the double strands of canvas and treating them as if they were single strands.

When stitching Petit Point, it is often easier to prick open the holes in the canvas before you start to stitch. Use a size bigger needle to gently move the canvas threads apart. Then when you start to stitch, you don't have to force the needle and thread through the canvas, which tends to wear the thread quickly. Also the stitches have a more even look when you take the time to pre-prick the canvas before you begin stitching.

Use a size 22 or 24 needle and any of the finer threads, Stranded Cotton (use 4-6 strands), Pearl 5 Cotton, Medici Wool (2-3 strands), to work Petit Point on Penelope canvas.

Try to work the stitches so that you go down into the smaller middle holes as shown in the diagram.

Try to work the stitches so that the needle goes **down** into the smaller middle holes

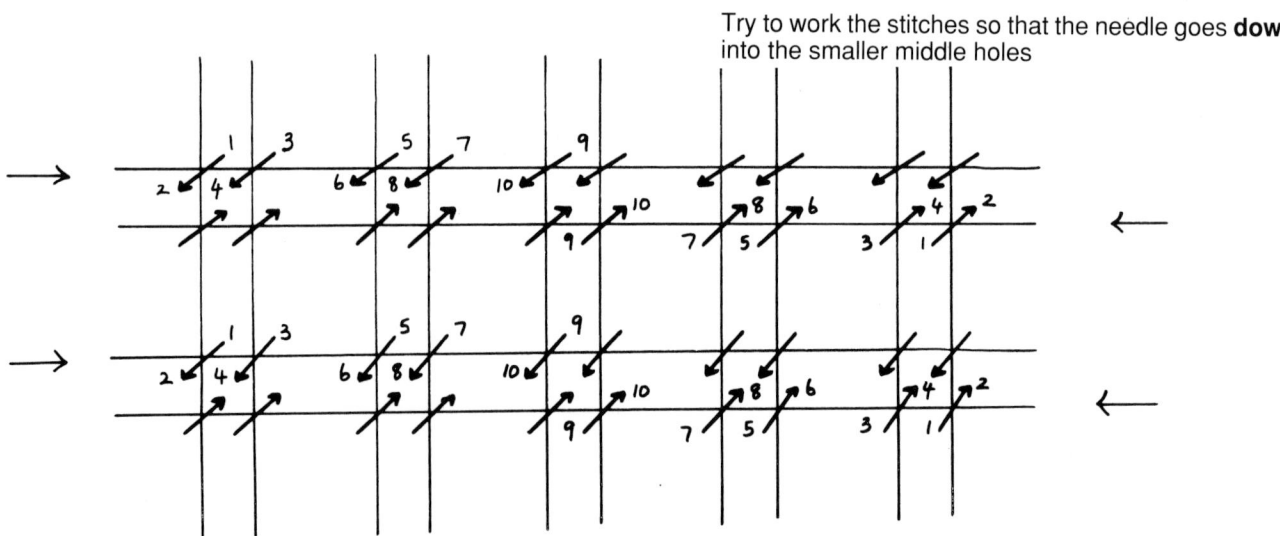

CANVAS CROSS STITCH

Canvas Cross Stitch is perhaps one of the most adaptable of the finer stitches used in Creative Tapestry. It is most effectively worked on Penelope Canvas because the double weave of the canvas allows the crossed effect of the stitch to be seen more clearly.

Use a size 22 tapestry needle and any of the finer threads, Stranded Cotton (use 6 strands), Pearl 5 Cotton or Medici wool, depending on the effect you want to create.

For Canvas Cross Stitch, first work a row of Reverse Continental Stitches, then work back over the *same* row with a row of Continental Stitches.

The most important factor with this stitch is that the top stitch slants to the *right*, that is, the same as Continental Stitch.

As well as being a perfect stitch for representing clothing, Canvas Cross Stitch can be used on buildings to give the texture of bricks; to give a smoother, more realistic look to the petals of flowers; or to highlight the lighter foliage on trees where the sun is shining through the leaves. It can even be used to work a complete background on a soft and dreamy design where a more washed-out effect is required than can be achieved by using any of the thicker threads.

First row

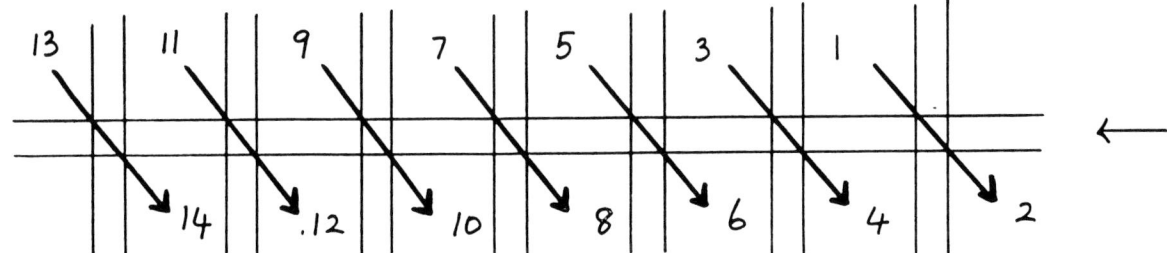

Second row worked over the first row

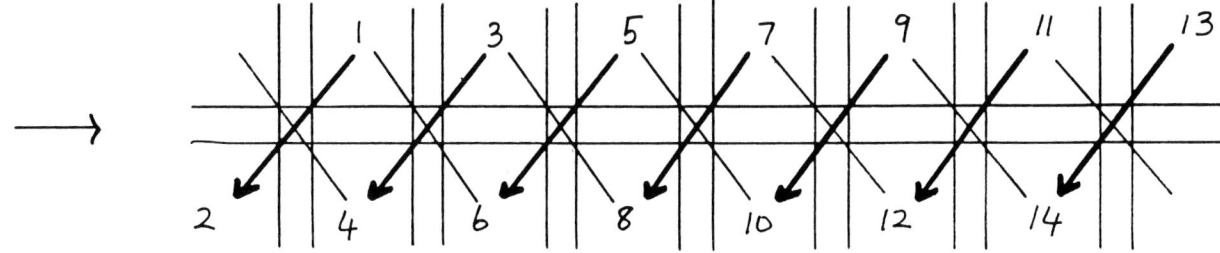

CANDLEWICKING KNOTS

Although we have already looked at Candlewicking Knots on Mono Canvas, it is worth mentioning that they can be used just as effectively on Penelope Canvas.

We usually work Candlewicking Knots on Penelope Canvas with a size 22 or 24 needle and the finer threads, such as Stranded Cotton (use 4-6 strands), Pearl 5 Cotton, Medici Wool, and maybe even Ribbon Floss, if a special effect is required.

To refresh your memory on how to do Candlewicking Knots, refer back to the section earlier in this chapter when we discussed Candlewicking Knots on Mono Canvas.

One important point to keep in mind when using any raised stitch in creative work, is to keep all the stitches used in proportion to each other so they all add to the realistic effect of the overall design. Creative work can be spoilt if one particular stitch seems to jump out at you when you look at the finished design. Rather, all the stitches and threads you use should work together to give the best overall finished effect.

Decorative and Background Stitches

Now that we have looked at some of the Basic Stitches we can use in designs on either Mono or Penelope Canvas, let us look at some of the more Decorative and Background Stitches that can be used on either type of canvas, single or double weave.

The diagrams show these stitches worked on Mono Canvas, but they can also be worked on Penelope Canvas. If you are using Penelope Canvas, work the stitches from large hole to large hole and then Petit Point hole to Petit Point hole (the hole between the double threads of canvas), continuing in this manner so that there is only one single thread of canvas between each stitch. This is necessary in order to cover the canvas properly.

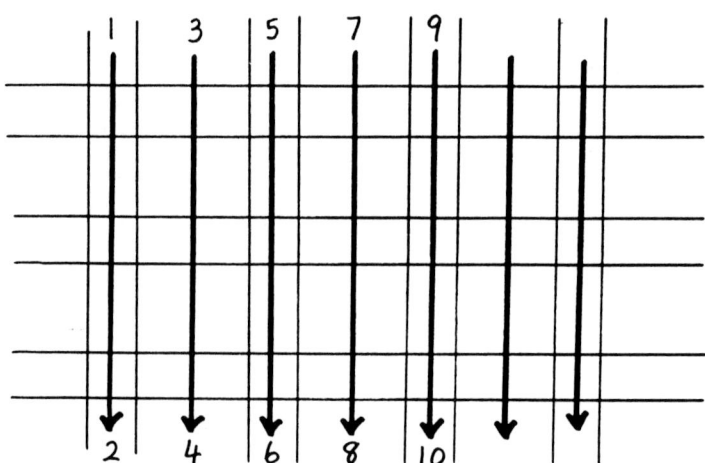

The Stitches 33

Tapestry Weaving Background, Candlewicking, Long Stitch, Double Cross Stitch.

Double Brick Background, Backstitching, Candlewicking Knits, Continental Stitch.

34 Creative Tapestry Made Easy

BASKETWEAVE STITCH

Unlike Continental Stitch, Basketweave Stitch does not bias and stretch the canvas. It is a very useful, hard-wearing stitch for use on large areas of background on cushions, chair covers, wall hangings, stool covers, etc.

Basketweave gets its name from the effect created on the wrong side of the canvas as you work, but it looks like Continental Stitch on the front of the work.

The difficult thing with Basketweave Stitch is to keep the correct stitching sequence up and down the diagonal. It takes some practise but stick with it and you will master the technique.

It can be difficult to keep the correct stitching sequence when you come to small areas between the main design features. When this happens you are best to revert back to Continental Stitches to fill in these areas.

PARISIAN STITCH

Parisian Stitch is another stitch suitable for larger areas and backgrounds. It is based on combinations of straight stitches of two varying lengths, with the larger stitch being three times the length of the smaller stitch. The stitches are alternated along the row, one long, one short, but on the next row the shorter stitches are worked under the longer stitches of the previous row.

Although usually worked using vertical straight stitches, there is no reason why it can't be worked using horizontal stitches, and if used for the background to a floral design, working the stitches

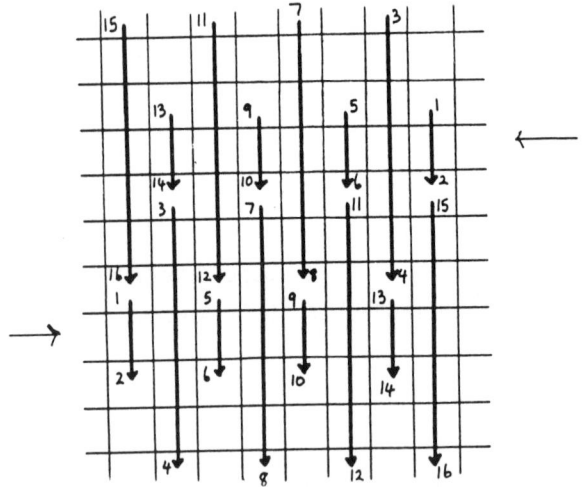

horizontally will recess the background more and help to make the main feature more prominent.

The usual size for working Parisian Stitch is with stitches over two and six canvas threads.

BRICK STITCH

Brick Stitch can be worked either vertically or horizontally, depending on the visual effect you want to create. The stitches are all the same length, but alternate stitches are staggered so that they begin halfway along the previous stitch. Although the stitch can be worked over any number of canvas threads, the larger version is usually worked over four threads and the smaller version over two threads.

Brick Stitch produces a very regular stitch, and care must be taken where it is used as it is a very prominent stitch. It must be used on a straight surface where decreasing in dimension or distance is

A smaller version of this stitch can also be worked if a finer, less chunky and lined effect is required. The smaller version is worked over one and three canvas threads.

not important.

Threads used, and the number of threads, will depend on the canvas size. Experiment until you get the coverage and look required. All the threads we have discussed so far can be used to stitch Brick Stitch, it only depends on the particular visual effect you want to create.

Brick Stitch can be worked by working alternate stitches across the row, or working two rows at once by staggering the stitches as you go. A diagram of both ways is included so you can choose the one that you find easiest to do.

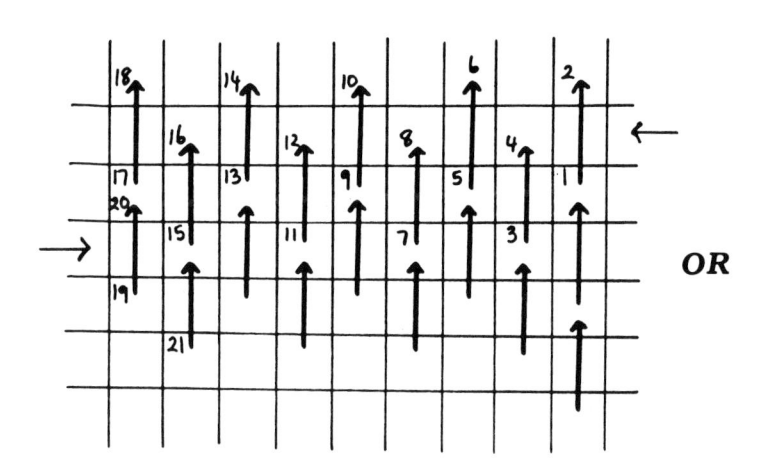

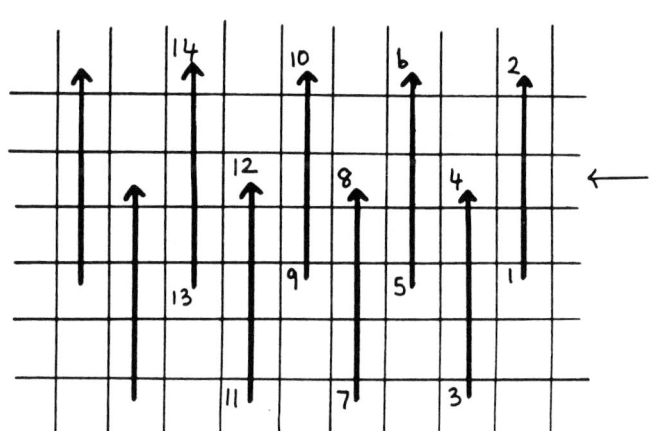

DOUBLE BRICK STITCH

This stitch is simply a variation of Brick Stitch where two stitches are worked instead of one before stepping up or down for the next stitch. This, of course, gives a chunkier look to the stitch which is usually worked in the thicker threads.

Although shown worked over four canvas threads here, smaller or larger versions can be stitched depending on the finished look required and the area to be covered.

Double Brick Stitch

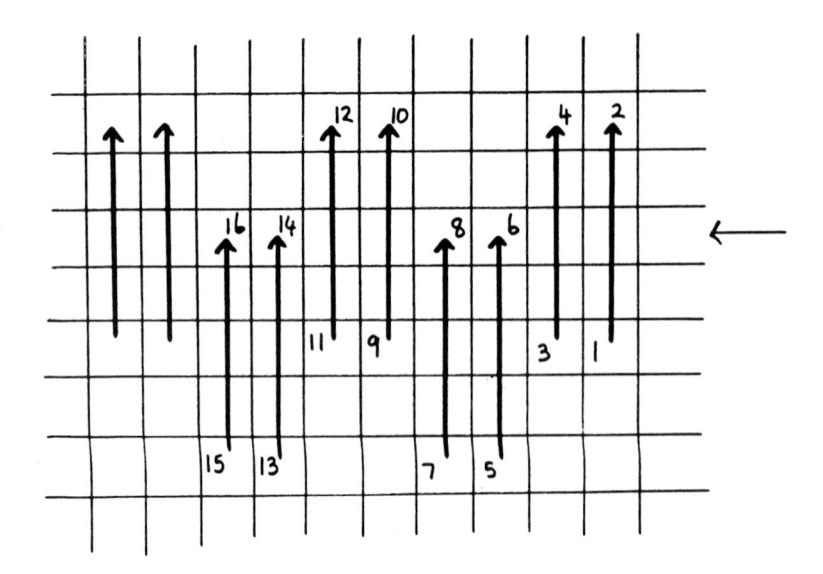

LARGE HORIZONTAL BRICK STITCH

This is another variation of Brick Stitch. Here the stitch is worked horizontally, and the length of the stitch is increased and worked over six canvas threads.

When working the stitches horizontally, it is easiest to work the rows up and down the canvas rather than across.

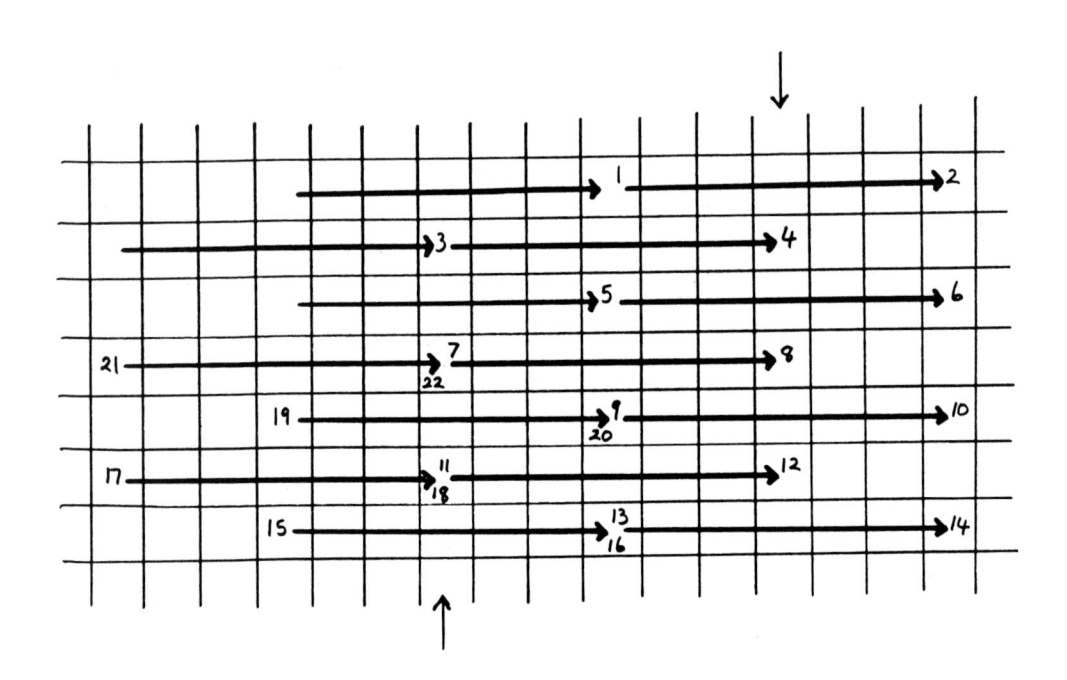

Parisian Stitch Background, Continental, Long Stitch, Double Cross, Candlewicking

TAPESTRY WEAVING STITCH

This is very much a novelty stitch we tried one day when we were looking for a reasonably quick-fill background stitch.

The stitch is worked simply by weaving the thread in and out of the canvas. It can be worked vertically or horizontally, and although it is shown here as going up and down between single canvas threads, there is no reason why you couldn't experiment with different combinations, eg over three under one strand.

Because the canvas actually shows in this stitch, the colour of the canvas used is important. You would probably only use the Weaving Stitch on white canvas, and when stitching in a pale colour of thread. It is best worked on Mono Canvas, where the canvas threads are evenly spaced apart.

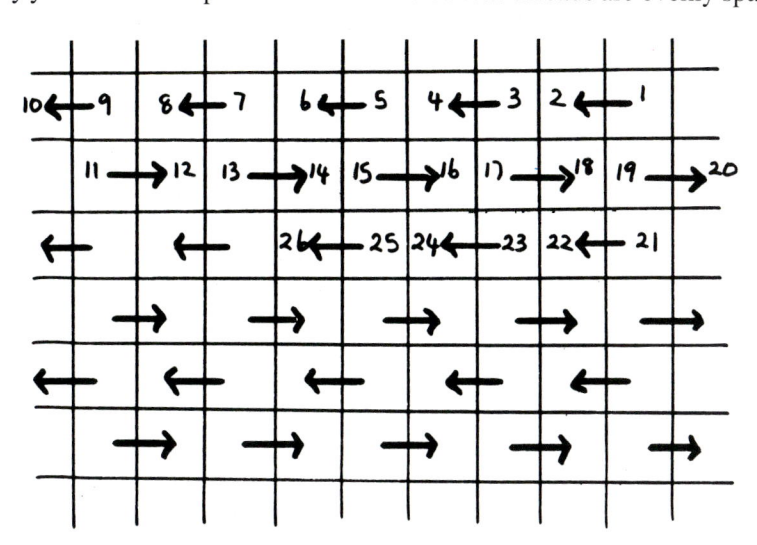

Extra Effect Stitches

The last two stitches we are going to look at are examples of *extra effect stitches*, extra stitches often placed within or on top of the stitching to give that little extra detail or effect.

BACKSTITCHING

Backstitching can be used to define lines, outline, or, for fine features such as whiskers. It can also be used to tidy up areas where two different stitches butt up to each other but do not cover completely.

Backstitch is best worked in finer threads, such as Stranded Cotton (4-6 strands) or Pearl 5 Cotton. Backstitching can be worked in any direction and each stitch is worked over one or two canvas threads.

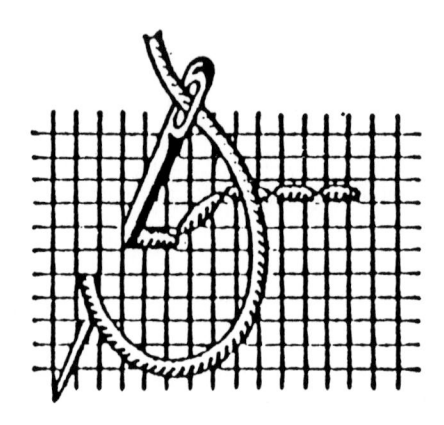

OVERSTITCHING

Overstitching is a technique of using long straight stitches, often placed in any direction, up, down, sideways or at any angle, to give extra dimension and definition to the design. Sometimes these stitches are placed first so that they outline a specific feature of the design such as a roof line, but more often they are placed over completed stitching to add extra interest, eg fences, vein of a leaf, long grass, branches of a tree, spokes of an umbrella, etc. Overstitching is a useful technique in all creative tapestry work as long as you remember to keep the length and thickness of the stitches in proportion to the other stitches used around the overstitching.

Large Horizontal Brick background, Candlewicking Knots, Double Cross , Continental Stitch, and Long Stitches.

Although these are by no means all the stitches that can be used in Creative Tapestry work, they do give a very good starting point. When combined with all the different threads we have discussed, they give you an extremely large number of variations to begin to use in your creative stitching.

It is important to remember that in Creative Tapestry it is not just the stitches, but rather the combinations of the correct stitches and threads that give your work that unique and individual look.

In the next chapter we show you how you can use these stitches in projects. The best way to get to know and feel confident with the different stitches is to practise them in a particular project.

40 Creative Tapestry Made Easy

4

CREATIVE TAPESTRY PROJECTS

We have chosen and designed projects that will allow you to practise with all the different threads and creative stitches we have talked about. Some projects are to be worked on different gauges of Mono Interlock Canvas and some on Double Weave Penelope Canvas, so that you can have experience with these different types of canvas and discover some of their possibilities and limitations.

The designs also show some of the versatility of creative canvas work, from a framed picture, to a modern floral bell pull, and a quick, easy and bright clown for a child's room. We have also included decor items for your home in the form of a doorstop cover, and a beautiful decor clock, as well as unique gift ideas or useful items for ourselves, with a wooden pin cushion and a glasses case.

The projects are the tip of the iceberg of possible Creative Tapestry projects, but we hope they give you ideas to help you practise and gain confidence. This, we hope, will then lead to many hours of stitching and creating your own masterpieces.

TRANSFERRING THE DESIGN OUTLINE TO THE CANVAS

It is very easy to transfer the design outlines to a canvas by following a few easy steps.

1 Make sure you have the correct type of canvas for the particular project you are doing, and that it is flat and without any wrinkles or creases that will affect the finished design. If necessary, press the canvas with an iron and a pressing cloth.

2 The canvas size we have suggested in each project leaves ample spare canvas around the stitched design so that you or your framer will have plenty

to work with when finishing off or framing your work. A little too much is always better than a little too little, especially when trying to stretch or block a design. Cut the canvas to the size stated for your chosen project.

3 Trace or photocopy the design outline from the book onto a large piece of paper, joining two sections where necessary so that the complete design is on one sheet of paper.

4 Position the canvas over the design outline sheet, making sure to **centre** the design in the middle of the canvas, leaving an equal amount of spare canvas around all four sides. Place something heavy on each corner of the canvas, or pin the canvas to the design sheet, to ensure neither the canvas nor the design sheet can move as you are tracing the design.

5 Using a very fine tipped permanent ink pen, trace the design onto the canvas carefully, making sure you complete one section at a time so no details are accidentally omitted.

When you think you have finished, compare the design on the canvas to the original outline in the book, before lifting the canvas from the design sheet, to double check that nothing has been omitted.

6 Now the design should be transferred clearly onto the canvas, and you are ready to attach the canvas to the working frame and begin stitching. Refer to Chapter 2 for how to stitch the canvas onto a frame.

Helpful Hint
Do NOT use a lead pencil to transfer the design to the canvas. When you later stitch up to the lines, the thread may pick up graphite from the lines and become soiled, which spoils the finished look of the project. Use a *very fine Overhead Projection Pen* which leaves a very fine, but easily seen line to follow as you stitch.

BEGINNING TO STITCH THE PROJECT

Before beginning to stitch your project, it is a good idea to spend a few minutes sorting out the threads and colours you are going to use to make sure you know which section is to be worked in which Creative Stitch, etc.

Helpful Hint
Sort the threads out into each section, eg background, flowers, leaves, walls, etc, and put the threads for each section in a separate plastic bag. With the threads put a note indicating which section the threads are for, and what stitches are to be used, eg Wall - Canvas Cross Stitch.

By organising yourself in this way, no valuable stitching time is wasted in looking up the correct colour, stitch, thread, etc, to be used. You can simply pick up the bag for the section you want and begin stitching.

ALTERNATIVE COLOUR SCHEMES

You will notice, as you read through the instructions for each project, that we have included alternative colour combinations for most of our projects. We realise that the colours we have chosen for our worked models may not be the ones to suit your taste or the decor of your home, so we hope that adding these extra colour schemes will enable you to find the perfect one for you.

QUICK REFERENCE OF HELPFUL HINTS AS YOU WORK

As you work your project, you may want to quickly refer back to sections of the book to refresh your memory on how to do a particular stitch, the length of thread to use, the easiest way to thread the needle, etc. Use the index, at the back of the book, to help you quickly find the information you wish to re-read. We have written the index so that it can be used by our readers as a ready reference for all those little bits of information and helpful hints that make your Creative Tapestry hours more enjoyable.

WOODEN PIN CUSHION

For the Pin Cushion we have given three different designs for you to choose from. The Pin Cushions are great gift ideas, and are good for using up left over threads.

MATERIALS

Wooden Pin Cushion Kit available from The Tapestry Guild (see Stockists)
20 cm (8 in) square of Mono Interlock Canvas, 70 threads/10 cm (18 holes/inch)
No 22 Tapestry Needle
15 cm (6 in) embroidery hoop (optional)

For the Pink Wave Pattern Design
(This is also the cover design.)
1 skein DMC Stranded Cotton, 3689
2 skeins of DMC Stranded Cotton, 819
1 skein of DMC Soft Cotton, 2574
1 skein of DMC Pearl 3 Cotton, 3689
1 roll of Soft Pink Ribbon Floss, Shade 11
1 roll of Pink Ice Metallic Ribbon Floss, Shade 8

For the Brick Stitch Variation Design
1 skein DMC Pearl 5 Cotton, 3687
1 skein DMC Pearl 5 Cotton, 3689

For the Floral Design
1 skein DMC Pearl 5 Cotton, 601
1 skein DMC Pearl 5 Cotton, 3689
1 skein DMC Pearl 5 Cotton, 604
1 skein DMC Stranded Cotton, 904
3 skeins DMC Soft Cotton, Ecru

INSTRUCTIONS

1 Remove the base plate from the centre of the wooden base by undoing the wing nut underneath.

Using the wooden circle as a pattern, draw around the circumference on your canvas lightly with a pencil. This will be a guide as to how far to carry out the design. You will need to *extend* the design area by at least 2 cm (3/4 in) all around the circle to allow for the padding that will go under the design.

2 Following the graph you have chosen, stitch the design onto the canvas.

It is easiest to begin all designs from the centre and work out, and we have marked the centre stitch on each graph.

For specific stitch directions, refer to Chapter 3.

Pink Wave Pattern Design
Each row is worked as per the graph, using a different thread for each row.

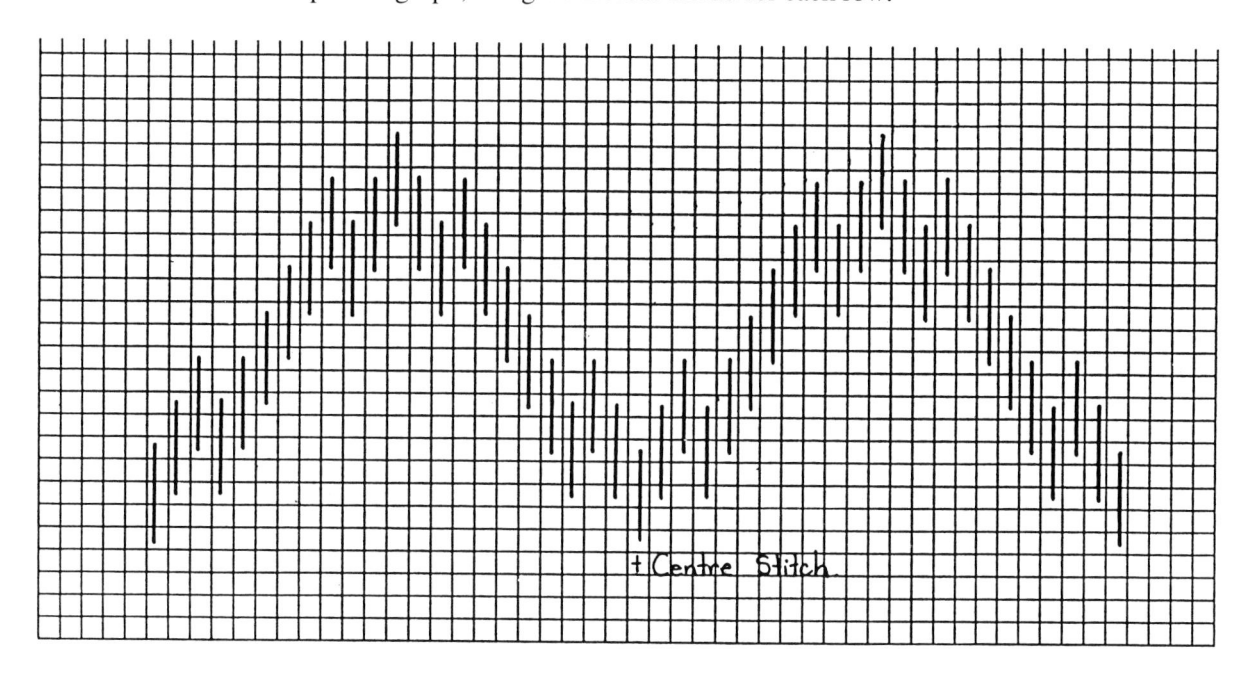

The sequence we used is:
1 row of Pearl 3 Cotton, 3689
1 row of Stranded Cotton, 819 (8 strands)
1 row of Blended Stranded Cotton, 4 strands each of 819 and 3689 used together (making a thickness of 8 strands)

1 row of Metallic Ribbon Floss, Pink Ice
1 row Soft Cotton, 2574
1 row Ribbon Floss, Soft Pink.

This sequence is repeated until the design area is covered.

Brick Stitch Variation

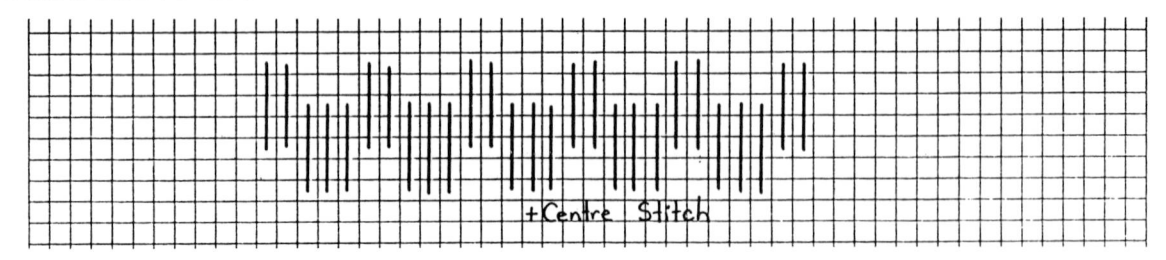

For this design Pearl 5 Cotton is used doubled throughout. The rows are worked as per the graph, and stitched in the following sequence:
1 row of darkest shade, 3687
1 row of lighter shade, 3689
1 row of Blended colours, 1 strand each of 3687 and 3689 worked together.

This sequence is repeated until the design is covered.

Floral Design

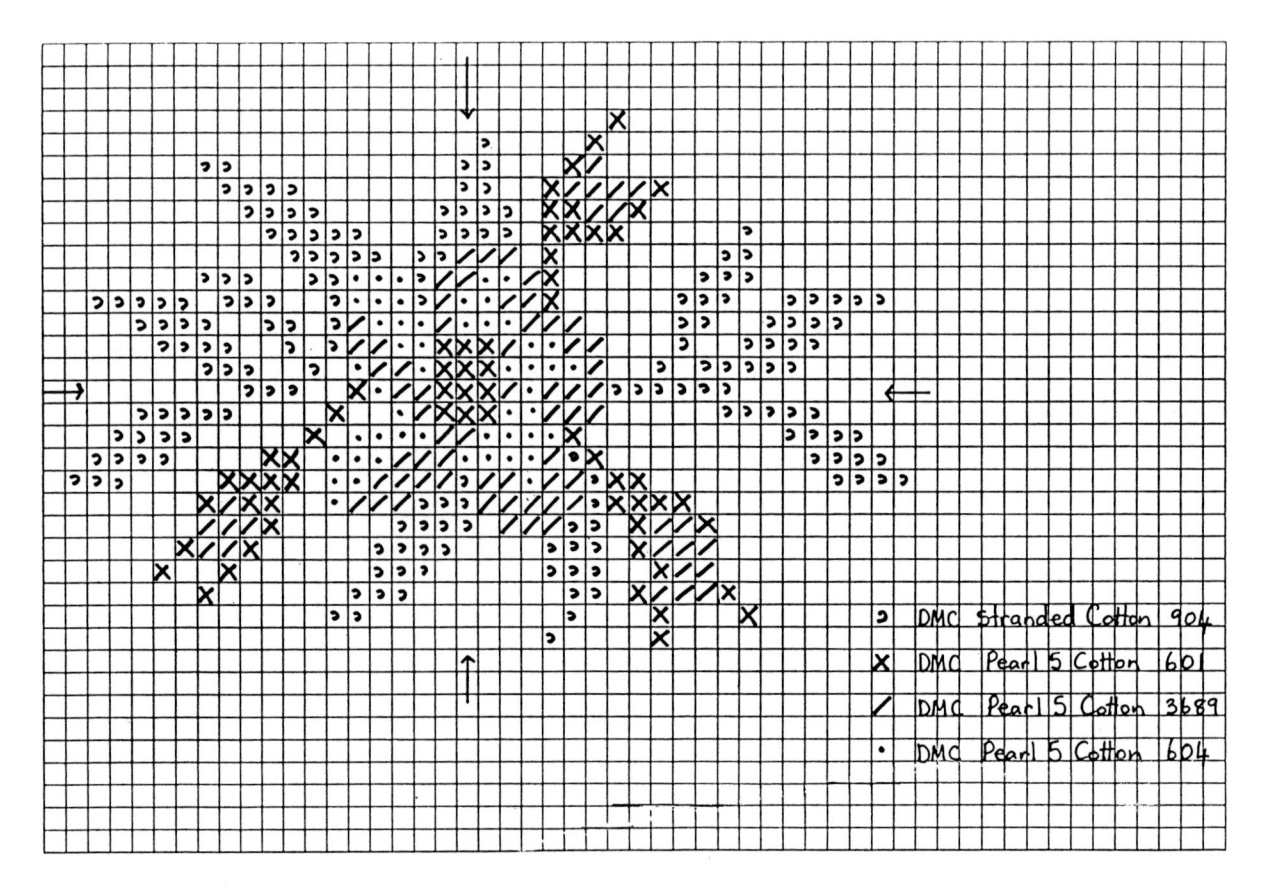

Use the graph to help you count this design onto the canvas. The main flower petals are worked in Candlewicking Knots. The centre of the flower is worked in Continental Stitch using Pearl 5 Cotton, to give the flowers a 3-dimensional look. The leaves and outer edges of the buds are also worked in Continental Stitch using Stranded Cotton (use 8 strands) and Pearl 5 Cotton. Check the key to the graph for correct colour placement.

The background to the design is then filled in with Soft Cotton (Ecru) in Continental or Basketweave Stitch. The use of a matt finish cotton for the background also helps to bring the flower, buds and leaves visually forward.

When you have completed stitching the design area, take the canvas out of the working frame and press it lightly on the wrong side of the work. Use a pressing cloth and a warm iron.

To assemble the design into the wooden base, refer to the directions given in Chapter 5.

46 Creative Tapestry Made Easy

DECOR DOOR STOP

Creative Tapestry Projects 47

DECOR DOOR STOP

In this project we have stitched a Creative Tapestry cover for an ordinary house brick, to make a doorstop which is not only decorative but very useful. We have stitched our model in modern peach tones, but we also give suggested colour schemes for pink and autumn tone versions.

MATERIALS

50 cm (20 in) square of Mono Interlock Canvas, 48 threads/10 cm (12 holes/inch)
2 skeins DMC Pearl 3 Cotton, 353
2 skeins DMC Pearl 3 Cotton, 352
1 skein DMC Stranded Cotton, 350
1 skein DMC Pearl 3 Cotton, 829
1 skein DMC Pearl 3 Cotton, 732
1 skein DMC Stranded Cotton, 936
2 skeins DMC Backgrounding Wool, Ecru, OR 10 skeins DMC Tapestry Wool, Ecru
No 20 Tapestry Needle
Tapestry Working Frame

INSTRUCTIONS

1 Mark the outline for your brick cover shape on your canvas following the diagram.

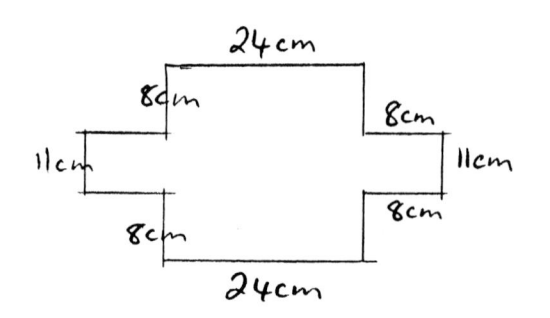

Place the outline so that it is 8 cm (3 in) from the top of the canvas, leaving extra canvas at the bottom of the outline to be used to cover the base of the brick when you make up the doorstop.

2 Using the design outline on page 46-47, transfer the design onto the canvas following the steps set out at the beginning of this chapter. Make sure you centre the design within the shape you have drawn on the canvas.

3 Sew the canvas onto a working frame and you are ready to start stitching.

For specific instructions on each stitch used, refer to the detailed stitch instructions in Chapter 3.

The flowers are worked in Candlewicking Knots with Pearl 3 Cotton, using the darker shade (352) for the outside of the petals, and the lighter shade (353) for the inner parts. The flowers are given a more 3-dimensional look by working their centres in Continental Stitch using Stranded Cotton (12 strands).

4 The main stems are worked in Pearl 3 Cotton (829) using Continental Stitch, and the finer stems are worked in the same thread and colour, but using Backstitch to get the curved, thin lines.

5 The leaves are worked in Continental Stitch using Pearl 3 Cotton (732), and the veins of the leaves are in Backstitched *over* the Continental Stitches using 4 strands of Stranded Cotton (936).

6 Finally, the background is filled in using Double Brick Stitch worked in Tapestry Wool (Ecru), to give a thick and durable finish to the design. When you stitch up to some areas of the design you will not be able to work complete Brick Stitches, so you will have to fill in with smaller straight stitches to cover any bare canvas.

Alternative Colour Schemes
If you would prefer pink tones or autumn (gold) tones for the doorstop, substitute the following:

Pink Tonings
   Petals - DMC Pearl 3 Cotton, 818, 899
   Centres of flowers - DMC Stranded Cotton, 815
   Stems - DMC Pearl 3 Cotton, 433

Autumn Tonings
   Petals - DMC PEARL 3 Cotton, 782, 783
   Centres of flowers - DMC Stranded Cotton, 919
   Stems - DMC Pearl 3 Cotton, 829
   Leaves - DMC Pearl 3 Cotton, 732 and Stranded Cotton, 936
   Background - DMC Tapestry Wool, 7746

   Leaves - DMC Pearl 3 Cotton, 989, and Stranded Cotton, 987
   Background - DMC Tapestry Wool, 7170

Remove the completed tapestry from the working frame. Press the work firmly on the wrong side, using a pressing cloth and a warm iron.

Full instructions for making up the doorstop and covering the house brick are found in Chapter 5.

50 Creative Tapestry Made Easy

MODERN FLORAL BELL PULL

Creative Tapestry Projects 51

MODERN FLORAL BELL PULL

In Victorian times, Bell Pulls were used to summon the servants, but nowadays they make an attractive decorator item. Making canvas work into a Bell Pull is an alternative to professional framing, and adds even more variety to the range of Creative Tapestry projects.

MATERIALS

32 cm x 50 cm (13 in x 20 in) of Mono Interlock Canvas, 70 threads/10 cm (18 holes/inch)
1 skein DMC Pearl 3 Cotton, 3345
2 skeins DMC Stranded Cotton, 3347
1 skein DMC Stranded Cotton, 3345
1 skein DMC Pearl 3 Cotton, 3347
2 skeins DMC Stranded Cotton, 3713
1 skein DMC Pearl 3 Cotton, 899
1 skein DMC Stranded Cotton, 3078
1 skein DMC Stranded Cotton, 899
14 skeins DMC Stranded Cotton, Ecru
No 20 Tapestry Needle
Tapestry Working Frame

INSTRUCTIONS

1 On the canvas, draw a rectangle 20 cm x 38 cm (8 in x 15 in), making sure to leave equal amounts of bare canvas around all four sides.

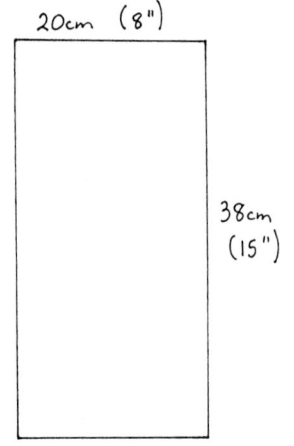

2 Using the design outline found on pages 50-51, transfer the design onto the canvas following the steps set out at the beginning of this chapter. Make sure you centre the design within the shape drawn on the canvas.

3 Sew the canvas onto a working frame and you are ready to start stitching.

For specific instructions on each stitch used, refer to the detailed stitch instructions in Chapter 3.

4 The outer border of the leaves are stitched in vertical Long Stitches using Pearl 3 Cotton, 3345; the centres of the leaves are stitched in Continental Stitch with Stranded Cotton, 3347 (use 6 strands); and the overstitched Backstitching on the leaves, used to represent the veins, is worked with Stranded Cotton, 3345 (use 4 strands).

5 The stems are worked in Horizontal Long Stitches using Pearl 3 Cotton, 3347.

6 The flowers have their outer borders stitched in Horizontal Long Stitches using Pearl 3 Cotton, 899, to outline the petal shapes. The centres are worked in Double Cross Stitch with Stranded Cotton, 3713 (use 6 strands). Some extra overstitched Backstitching has been added to the petals using Stranded Cotton 899 (6 strands). This gives the illusion of the petals opening out and also helps to recess the centre of the flower, giving a more 3-dimensional look to the flowers.

7 The centres of the flowers are worked in Candlewicking Knots with Stranded Cotton, 3078, using 6 strands and a No 22 needle. Some extra Candlewicking Knots are worked over the Double Cross Stitch of the petals and joined to the centre with a joining Backstitch, to add extra interest to the flowers.

8 For the background we used Large Horizontal Brick Stitch, worked with Stranded Cotton (use 8 strands), colour Ecru. We purposely used a Horizontal stitch because stitches worked horizontally give a more recessed look than those worked vertically. This allows the main feature of the project, the flowers, to come forward visually and give a more pleasing effect.

Remove the completed tapestry from the working frame and press the stitching firmly on the wrong side, using a pressing cloth and a warm iron. The full instructions for making the worked canvas into a beautiful Bell Pull to hang on the wall are found in Chapter 5.

54 Creative Tapestry Made Easy

COLOURFUL, NOVELTY CLOWNS

Creative Tapestry Projects 55

COLOURFUL, NOVELTY CLOWNS

Colourful Clowns use a variety of different Creative Stitches and threads to make a bright and decorative picture for any child's room. The stitched canvas can be either professionally framed or, you can frame it yourself in an inexpensive flexihoop.

MATERIALS

40 cm (16 in) square of Mono Interlock Canvas, 56 threads/10 cm (14 holes/inch)
No 20 Tapestry Needle
No 22 Tapestry Needle

For the Bright Multi-coloured Clown
2 skeins DMC Stranded Cotton, 3078
3 skeins DMC Stranded Cotton, Ecru
1 skein DMC Stranded Cotton, 350
1 skein DMC Pearl 3 Cotton, 973
2 skeins DMC Pearl 3 Cotton, 971
1 skein DMC Pearl 3 Cotton, 907
1 skein DMC Pearl 5 Cotton, 973
3 skeins DMC Tapestry Wool, 7666
5 skeins DMC Tapestry Wool, 7318

Scrap of DMC Stranded Cotton 825 (dark blue)

For the Pink Clown
1 skein DMC Stranded Cotton, 927
3 skeins DMC Stranded Cotton, 225
2 skeins DMC Stranded Cotton, 3354
1 skein DMC Pearl 3 Cotton, 3687
2 skeins DMC Pearl 3 Cotton, White
1 skein DMC Pearl 3 Cotton, 3689
1 skein DMC Pearl 5 Cotton, 3687
2 skeins DMC Pearl 5 Cotton, 818
3 skeins DMC Tapestry Wool 7205
Scrap of DMC Stranded Cotton 415 (pale grey) & 814 (maroon)

INSTRUCTIONS

1 Draw a circle 25 cm (10 in) in diameter on the canvas, making sure to centre the circle in the middle of the piece of canvas.

2 Using the design outline found on pages 54-55, transfer the design onto the canvas following the steps set out at the beginning of this chapter. Make sure you centre the design within the shape drawn on the canvas.

3 Sew the canvas onto a working frame and you are ready to start stitching.

For specific instructions on each stitch used, refer to the detailed stitch instructions in Chapter 3.

4 In the following instructions the colour numbers shown are for the Bright Multi-coloured Clown while the numbers in brackets are for the Pink Clown.

The face, eyes and mouth are all worked in Continental Stitch using Stranded Cotton (8 strands) Ecru, 350, 3078 (225, white).

For extra definition, the eyes and mouth are backstitched around, as are the centre of the mouth and the cross in the centre of each eye, using scraps of Stranded Cotton (2 strands), 825 (eyes, 415 pale grey, and cross in eyes and mouth, 814 maroon).

5 The nose is filled in with Candlewicking Knots using a Size 22 needle and Pearl 5 Cotton, 973 (3687).

6 The collar of the clown's suit is worked in Double Cross Stitch with Stranded Cotton (6 strands) 3078 (3354).

7 The frill around the edge of the collar is worked in Candlewicking Knots this time using a Size 20 needle and Pearl 3 Cotton, 907 (white).

8 The clown's suit and eyebrows are stitched with Vertical Long Stitches in Tapestry Wool 7666 (7205).

9 Extra interest is added to the hair by working it in Candlewicking Knots using a Size 20 needle and Pearl 3 Cotton. On the Multi-coloured Clown we mixed two colours, 973 and 971, and for the Pink

Clown only white was used.

10 The hat is worked in stripes of Vertical Long Stitches with Pearl 3 Cotton, 907 and Tapestry Wool 7666 (Pearl 3 Cotton, 3689 & Tapestry Wool 7205).

11 The pom pom is again worked in Candlewicking Knots to balance the use of textures in the design. Pearl 3 Cotton is used with a Size 20 needle and two colours randomly mixed, 973, 971 (white, 3687).

12 We used different backgrounds on our clowns to show the effects that can be achieved with different stitches. On the Multi-coloured Clown we have a solid, heavy texture achieved by using Vertical Parisian Stitch worked over two and 6 canvas threads in Tapestry Wool, 7318. For the Pink Clown we have a lacy, softer and more delicate look formed by using Tapestry Weaving Stitch worked in a pastel shade of Pearl 5 Cotton, 818.

FRAMING THE NOVELTY CLOWNS

There are two different ways the stitched Clown designs can be framed.

Remove the completed designs from the working frame. Press the work firmly on the wrong side, using a pressing cloth and a warm iron. Take care not to flatten the Candlewicking Knots too much, but give the face and background areas a good press.

We had one of our designs professionally framed with a matt surround and a narrow frame. In Chapter 5 there is a list of hints on how a framer should handle your canvases, and we suggest you discuss some of these points with him before leaving your work to be framed.

Alternatively, you may wish to frame the design yourself. Our Pink Clown has been framed in an inexpensive Flexihoop, with a lace and material ruffle added for extra effect. Full instructions for this method can be found in Chapter 5.

AUTUMN LEAVES TAPESTRY CLOCK

The beauty of the unique Tapestry Clock lies in the simplicity of its design.

MATERIALS

40 cm (16 in) square of Penelope Canvas (double weave), 39 threads/10 cm (10 holes/inch)
1 skein DMC Pearl 3 Cotton, 581
1 skein DMC Pearl 3 Cotton, 580
1 skein DMC Pearl 3 Cotton, 832
1 skein DMC Pearl 3 Cotton, 301
1 skein DMC Pearl 3 Cotton, 975
1 skein DMC Pearl 3 Cotton, 976
20 skeins DMC Stranded Cotton, Ecru
No 20 Tapestry Needle
Gold Metallic Floss, or similar, for hour dashes

INSTRUCTIONS

1 On the canvas, draw a 30 cm (11.5 in) circle, making sure to centre it in the middle of the piece of canvas.

2 Sew the canvas onto a working frame, and you are ready to start stitching.

For specific instructions on each stitch used, refer to the detailed stitch instructions in Chapter 3.

3 This design is worked from the coloured graph on page 60.

Each square on the graph represents the intersection of the canvas threads. For the leaves each square represents one Continental Stitch, and for the background each square represents one Canvas Cross Stitch. Before you begin stitching, mark the centre square of the circle on the canvas. This stitch is also marked on the graph, and all the counting should be done from this stitch.

4 The leaves of the design are all worked in Continental Stitch in Pearl 3 Cotton. Refer to the key of the graph for which colours to use on each leaf.

5 Once all the leaves have been stitched, the background can be filled in with Canvas Cross Stitch in Stranded Cotton (6 strands), Ecru. DO NOT stitch the centre stitch and the four surrounding stitches marked on the graph. This is where the spindle that the hands are attached to, will come through the canvas when you make up the clock.

6 Once the background is completed, stitch in the the hour dashes, following the positions marked on the graph. The 12, 3, 6 and 9 hour dashes are worked in Cross Stitches over the background stitching. We have used Gold Metallic Ribbon Floss, but any gold metallic thread of similar thickness would be suitable. All the other hour dashes are stitched with slanted lines of three backstitches.

When all the stitching has been completed, take the design off the working frame. Press it lightly on the wrong side using a pressing cloth. If necessary, gently pull it back into shape as you press.

Instructions for assembling the Tapestry Clock are found in Chapter 5.

60 Creative Tapestry Made Easy

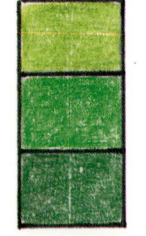

	DMC Pearl 3 – 976		DMC Pearl 3 – 832
	DMC Pearl 3 – 301		DMC Pearl 3 – 581
	DMC Pearl 3 – 975		DMC Pearl 3 – 580

Creative Tapestry Projects 61

Autumn Leaves Tapestry Clock

Wave Pattern Glasses Case

62 Creative Tapestry Made Easy

Wave Pattern Design

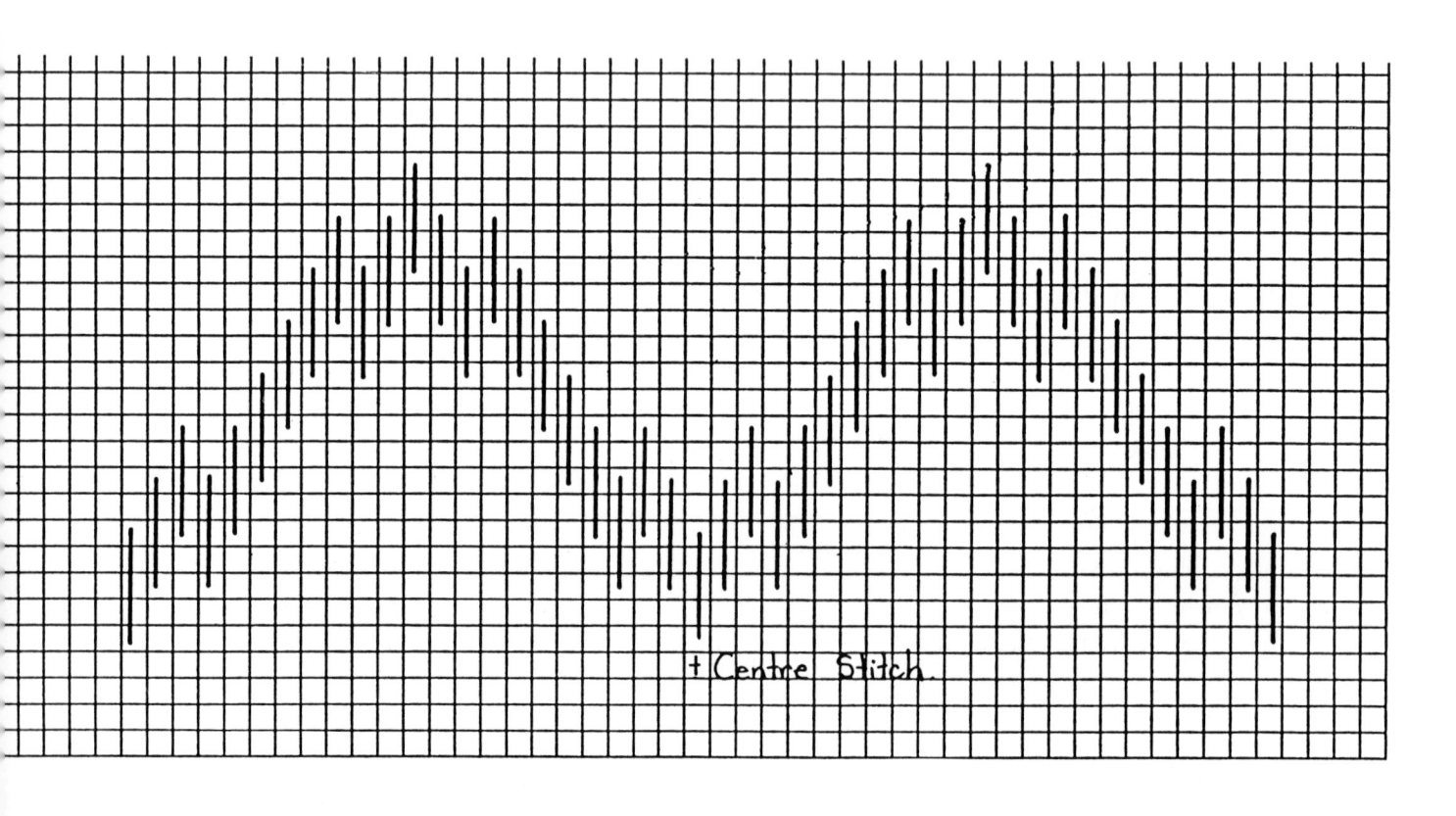

† Centre Stitch.

WAVE PATTERN GLASSES CASE

This is the cover design again, used to make a very stylish but useful Glasses Case. We stitched our case in shades of gold, but you could use the same tones of pink used in the Pink Wave Pattern Pin Cushion, or the suggested colours for working a silver/grey or blue version.

MATERIALS

16 cm x 48 cm (6 1/2 in x 19 in) of Mono Interlock Canvas, 70 threads/10 cm (18 holes/inch)
1 skein DMC Medici Wool, 8326
1 skein DMC Pearl 3 Cotton, 676
1 skein DMC Pearl 5 Cotton, 729
1 skein DMC Pearl 5 Cotton, 676
3 skeins DMC Stranded Cotton, 676
1 roll Ribbon Floss, yellow shade 25
1 roll Metallic Ribbon Floss, gold
Tapestry Working Frame
No 20 Tapestry Needle

INSTRUCTIONS

1 Draw a rectangle 9 cm x 39 cm (3 1/2 x 15 in), making sure you centre the rectangle on the piece of canvas. Draw across the rectangle halfway along each long side.
2 Sew the canvas onto the working frame. Following the graph given for the Pink Wave Pattern Pin Cushion, work each row with a different thread using the following sequence:
1 row Medici Wool
1 row Ribbon Floss
1 row Pearl 3 Cotton
1 row Metallic Ribbon Floss
1 row Stranded Cotton (use 8 strands)
1 row Pearl 5 Cotton (use 1 strand of each shade of Pearl 5 Cotton worked together).
3 We worked our Glasses Case exactly three patterns wide. The direction of the stitching was changed at the halfway point so that the side seams would match up when sewed together, but you don't have to do this if you find it easier to work all the one way.

You will need to fill in the gaps at each end with part rows until all the stitching ends on the one row of canvas. Take care to keep the sequence of threads correct.

Alternative colour schemes for the Glasses Case
A silver/grey design can be worked by stitching the rows in the following sequence in the threads suggested.
1 row DMC Pearl 3 Cotton, 318
1 row Metallic Ribbon Floss, silver
1 row DMC Medici Wool, 8509
1 row DMC Stranded Cotton, 415
1 row DMC Pearl 5 Cotton, blend of 415 and 414
1 row Ribbon Floss, shade 27
A blue design can be worked by stitching the rows in the following sequence in the threads suggested.
1 row DMC Pearl 3 Cotton, 322
1 row Metallic Ribbon Floss, shade 9
1 row DMC Medici Wool, 8209
1 row DMC Pearl 5 Cotton, blend of 3325 and 775
1 row Ribbon Floss, Pale Blue shade 21
1 row Stranded Cotton, 3755

When you have completed stitching the design, you may need to press it lightly on the wrong side. Use a pressing cloth and a warm iron, and gently pull it back into shape if necessary, as you press.

For information on making up and lining the Glasses Case, refer to the directions in Chapter 5.

64 Creative Tapestry Made Easy

5

FINISHING TECHNIQUES

HINTS FOR HAVING COMPLETED WORKS PROFESSIONALLY FRAMED

By the time you have finished your tapestry you will have put in many hours of careful and loving stitching, so it deserves to be framed correctly.

The framing of the tapestry should show your work off to its best advantage so don't be afraid to take the time to carefully choose a frame that best suits the colours and theme of the tapestry. Think about where you are going to hang your tapestry, the frames on the other pictures in the room, the type of furniture in the room (modern, antique), wall colours, curtains, etc.

Some students have asked why we don't frame our work ourselves. We have watched framers at work, and have noted the expertise and special equipment needed to ensure a professional finish to a frame. We know we could not achieve the same effect, so we are happy to take our work to an expert.

When deciding on which framer to go to, it is often helpful to ask around among your friends and look at some of the work they have already had framed. Has the tapestry been stretched so that it is straight and tight with no lumps, bumps, loose areas or waves in the rows of stitches?

Unfortunately, over the years, we have seen several tapestries ruined by careless framing and so we suggest to our students that before they leave their tapestries to be framed, they ask a few questions about how their work will be handled.

It is better to speak up now than be sorry later.

The following ideas are ones you should keep in mind when talking to your framer -

1 NEVER put glass in front of your tapestry. It will flatten the stitches and, as glass generates heat, it will fade the threads. You use natural fibres to work your tapestry and glass will prevent them from breathing. Also, it will trap moisture which, over a period of time, will ROT the canvas.
2 Make sure your Framer only STAPLES your tapestry to the backing board, and does not glue it, so that if necessary it can be taken off the board. Make sure he DOES NOT cut off any excess canvas.
3 Have your tapestry padded with *polyester wadding*, not foam, as foam breaks down over time.
4 Your tapestry should not be moistened before it is stretched or blocked, especially if it contains silk or metallic threads. If you work the tapestry on a solid lap working frame, it should not need a great amount of stretching before it is mounted on its backing board.

You can Scotchguard your completed work before it is framed if you wish, but special care should be taken if you have used metallic threads and/or beads. When spraying with Scotchguard, give a light spray on the back of the work, then on the front, then on the back again. Several light sprays are much better than one heavy one.

DO NOT SATURATE the tapestry as some of the colours may tend to run.

As a final touch, you can also ask the framer to put a thin strip of foam on the bottom of the back of the frame, or small plastic corner mounts, so that when you finally hang your tapestry on the wall it will not slip and will hang straight.

66 Creative Tapestry Made Easy

ASSEMBLING THE WOODEN BASE PIN CUSHION

When you have stitched and pressed your tapestry top for the Pin Cushion, it is time to put it into the wooden base.

MATERIALS

Wooden Pin Cushion Kit (available from The Tapestry Guild)
Canvas design, stitched and pressed
Needle and spare thread
Craft Glue
Scissors to trim canvas
35 cm (14 in) narrow braid
Small 3 mm (1/8 in) ribbon bow to match braid

INSTRUCTIONS

1 Cut around the design, leaving at least 2 cm (1 in) of spare canvas.

2 With some spare thread, run a gathering stitch around the edges of the canvas. Later, this will be used to tighten the canvas around the base plate.

3 Make sure that the screw is in the base plate that has been taken out of the top of the wooden base. Lightly glue the piece of foam that comes with the base onto the base plate to prevent it from slipping.

4 Place the worked design UPSIDE DOWN on a flat surface, then place the foam and base plate on top of the design. Carefully pull the gathering thread to draw the canvas firmly over the base plate.

5 When you are satisfied with the fit of the canvas over the base plate and have smoothed out the gathers around the canvas, lace the canvas across the back firmly, or use a staple gun, to hold the canvas in position.

6 Turn the base plate, which is now covered with the design, over and place it back into the wooden base.

7 Tighten the screw through the centre hole using the nut provided. A small pair of pliers may be handy.

8 To finish off, and add that little extra touch, the braid can be glued around the outer edge of the design and the top of the wooden base. Finish off with a small bow to conceal the join in the braid.

MAKING UP THE TAPESTRY BELL PULL

There are times when we do not want to frame our tapestry work, and would prefer to make it into a narrow wall hanging or a Bell Pull.

When working a tapestry that you want to finish off by making it into a Bell Pull, there are a few things to keep in mind. It is important to keep the work as square as possible as it is stitched. Always work on a rigid working frame. This will also protect the canvas which is the foundation of your work.

When choosing the stitches you are going to use in the piece, be careful to use those which will not bias, or stretch the work out of shape. For example, if you want a plain background, use Basketweave rather than Continental stitch. If using decorative stitches, use those made up of vertical and horizontal stitches rather than diagonal stitches, which do have a tendency to stretch the canvas sideways as they are worked.

MATERIALS REQUIRED

Design, stitched and pressed
50 cm (18 in) medium weight backing material
Iron-on Vylene, same size as design area
Pair of ornate metal Bell Pull ends, 20 cm (8 in) wide
Machine thread in the same colour as the stitched background
Invisible thread
Scissors to trim canvas
Sewing machine for sewing on backing material

INSTRUCTIONS

Before you begin to sew the material backing onto the completed tapestry, make sure it has remained straight. If it hasn't, you may need to have the work blocked by a framer. To keep your work straight, it is helpful to iron interfacing onto the back of the completed canvas to stop it from 'moving' when it is hung. Referring to the numbered diagrams, proceed as follows:

1 Trim the canvas so that there is a little over 1 cm (3/8 in) of raw canvas around the stitched design.

2 Cut some medium weight backing fabric, such as imitation suede or plain furnishing fabric, to the same size as the trimmed canvas. Make sure that the colour of the backing material blends with the colours used in the tapestry.

3 Cut two smaller pieces of fabric the same width as the backing fabric and 5 cm (2 in) long.

4 With right sides together, sew the smaller pieces of fabric to each narrow end of the canvas. When sewing, have the canvas facing upwards so that one stitch can be sewn inside the edge of the work.

5 With the right sides of the stitched design and the backing piece together, sew the side seams to within 2 cm (3/4 in) of each end. Again, have the canvas facing up as you sew, and sew one stitch inside the edge of the stitching. Trim the side seams, then turn the work right side out.

6 Using invisible thread, or one that matches the background thread, top stitch the side seams close to the edge (about 2mm [1/16 in]) to flatten the seam. A good press at this stage may be useful, depending on the mediums used in the stitching. Use a pressing cloth to avoid damaging the threads.

Hand stitch the raw edges of the sides left open at

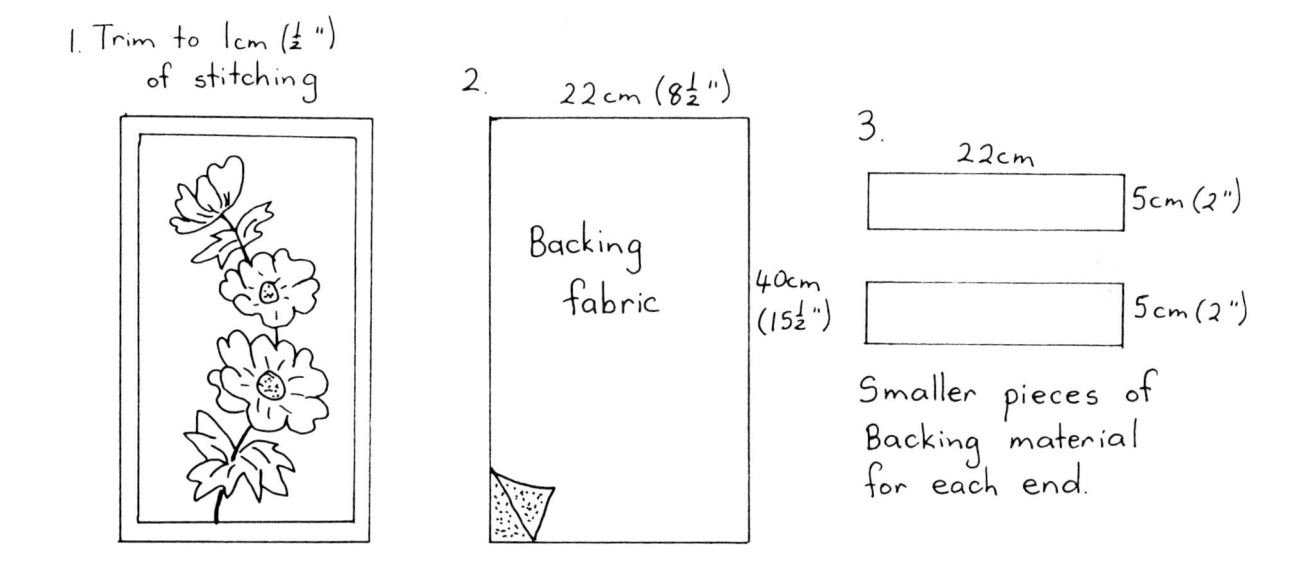

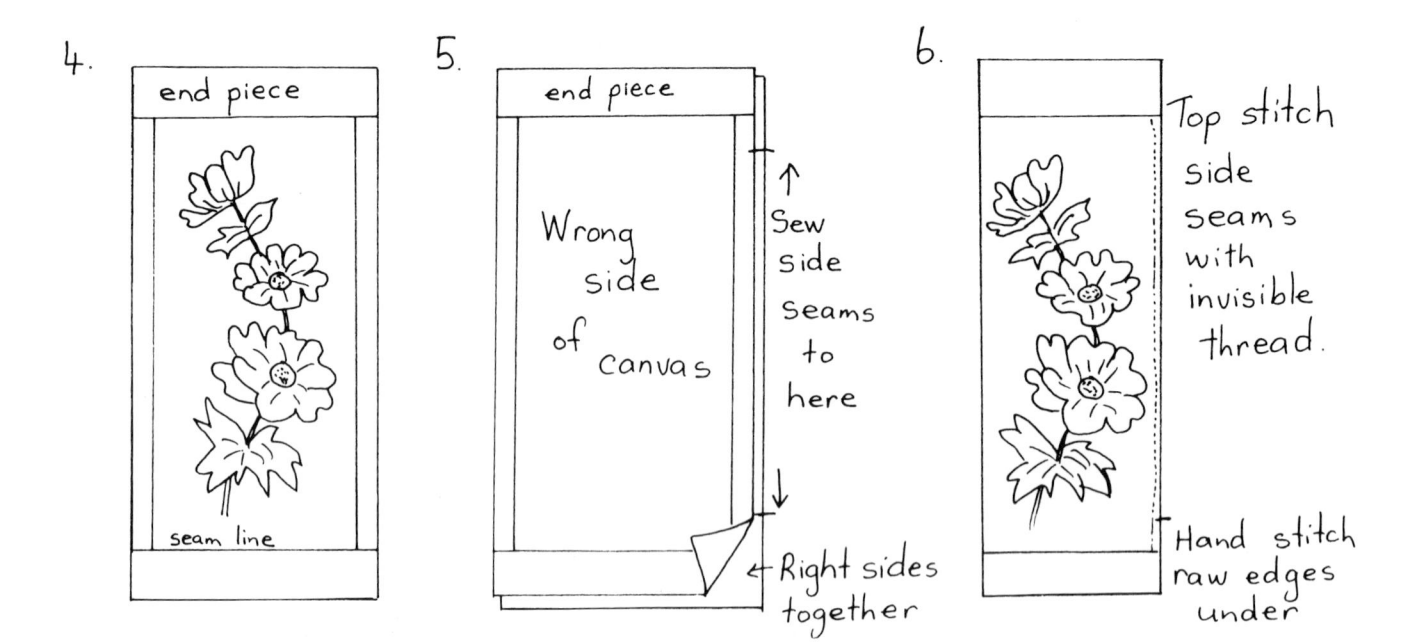

4. end piece / seam line

5. end piece / Wrong side of canvas / Sew side seams to here / Right sides together

6. Top stitch side seams with invisible thread. / Hand stitch raw edges under

each end on both the canvas and the backing material.

7 Attach the work to the metal ends. Using the short pieces of fabric as a lever, pull the end of the canvas up through, and back down over, the bar on the back or bottom of the Bell Pull fitting.

8 Turn under the raw edge of the backing fabric and hand stitch the edges together, thus enclosing the metal bar. Repeat the same process at the other end of the tapestry.

The Bell Pull is complete and ready to hang.

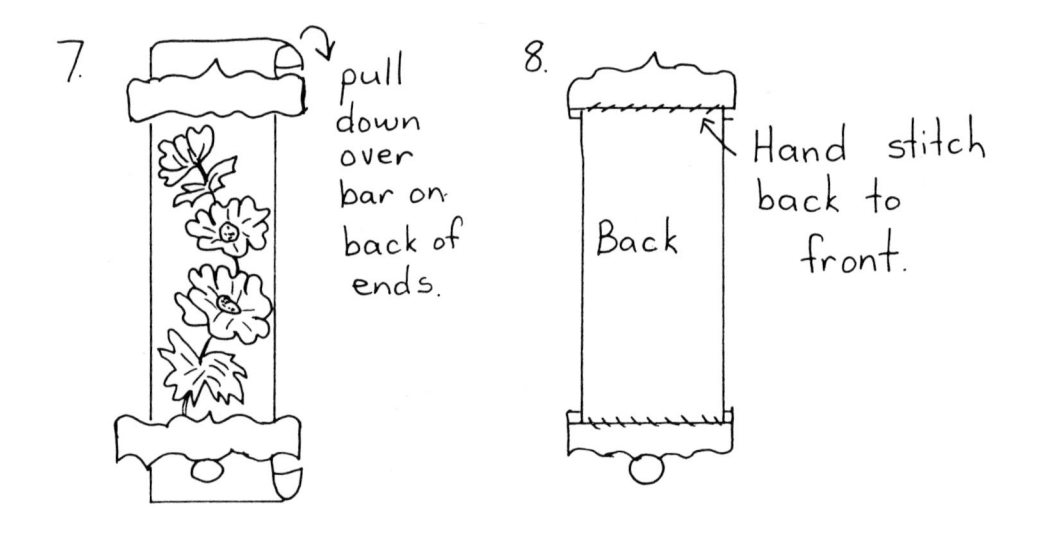

7. pull down over bar on back of ends.

8. Back / Hand stitch back to front.

MAKING UP THE DECOR DOORSTOP

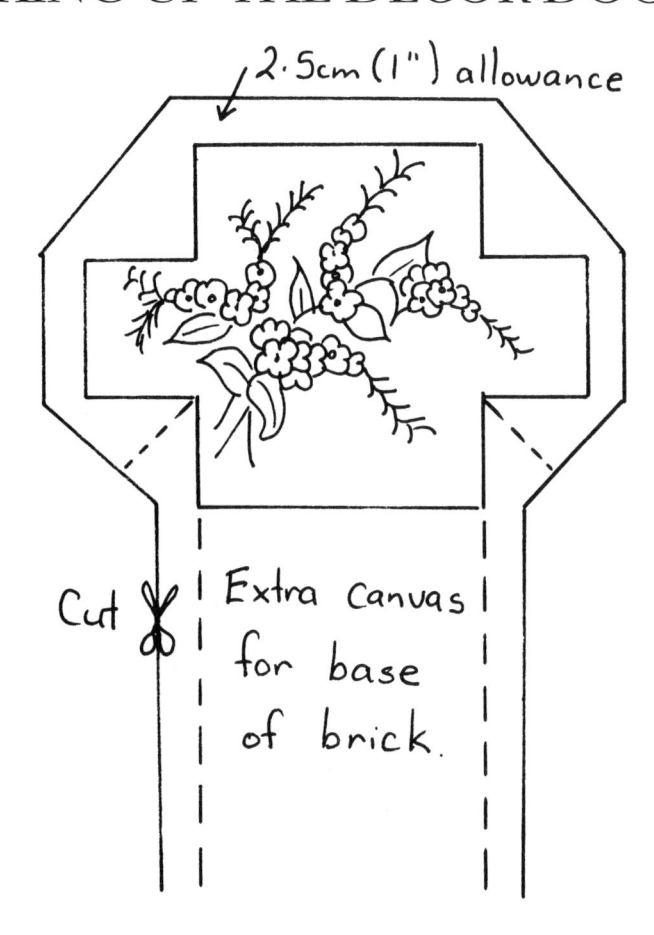

2.5cm (1") allowance

Cut — Extra canvas for base of brick.

When you have stitched the tapestry covering, it is time to cover an ordinary brick and make it into a decorative and practical Doorstop.

MATERIALS

One standard house brick
50cm (20 in) square polyester wadding
25 cm x 15 cm (10 in x 6 in) grey felt
Nylon invisible thread

Pins
Craft glue
Scissors to trim canvas

INSTRUCTIONS

1 Trim the canvas around the edges to within 2.5 cm (1 in) of the stitching. The corners will need to be cut on the diagonal. Remember to leave one extra long side to cover the bottom of the brick.
2 The brick needs to be covered with wadding before the worked tapestry is attached. Cut six pieces of wadding, each to the size of the sides of the brick, and glue into position using the craft glue.
3 Place the padded brick onto the wrong side of the worked tapestry. Carefully fold the sides of the

tapestry around the brick, pinning into place as you go. Fold the excess canvas at the corners to the inside of the cover. The sides of the stitched tapestry should butt up against each other down the corners of the brick. Blind stitch the corners together using invisible nylon thread.

4 When all four corners have been stitched together, pull the excess unworked canvas for the base over the bottom of the brick. Tuck under any excess canvas (trim where necessary), and blind stitch around the three unsewn edges of the base.

5 Cut the felt to the size of the bottom of the brick and glue in place using Craft Glue.

ASSEMBLING A TAPESTRY IN A FLEXIHOOP

We have chosen a different way of framing one of our Clown Designs to give you an alternative to professional framing. This method uses a 25 cm (10 in) wooden embroidery hoop, enhanced by the addition of a material ruffle, lace, braid and ribbon.

MATERIALS REQUIRED

25 cm (10 in) Wooden Embroidery Hoop
10 cm x 120 cm (4 in x 48 in) material for ruffle
1 m (1 yd) x .5 cm (1/4 in) braid
25 cm (10 in) circle of stiff cardboard

1 m (1 yd) pre-gathered lace
Craft glue
Short length of ribbon

INSTRUCTIONS

1 Trim the canvas to within approximately 2.5 cm (1 in) of the stitched area.

2 Undo the screw from the top of the embroidery hoop, and place the tapestry over the inner circle of the hoop. Place the outside ring over the tapestry, adjusting it to fit and making sure to line up the tapestry into the correct position.

3 When you are satisfied with the fit, tighten the screw, and put it aside while you sew the ruffle. Fold excess canvas towards the centre of the hoop.

4 Fold and press the length of material for the ruffle in half lengthways. On the two short ends, fold in the raw edges about 1 cm (1/2 in). Run a gathering thread along the bottom raw edge and gather the material up until it fits the circumference of the hoop.

5 Glue the pre-gathered lace to the back of the hoop, around the outside edge. Then glue the ruffle behind the lace to give a pretty, soft effect.

6 To neaten the back of your hoop and also to keep the light out, glue the cardboard circle to the back of the hoop. This will hide any excess canvas and the raw edge of the ruffle.

7 Glue the braid to the front of the wood that is showing around the outside of the design.

8 Make a ribbon loop and tie it with a bow around the tightening screw at the top of the picture. This loop can be used to hang the finished project.

74 Creative Tapestry Made Easy

ASSEMBLING YOUR TAPESTRY CLOCK

MATERIALS

26 cm (10 in) circular wooden frame
Backing Board to fit circular frame
1 clock movement
1 set of clock hands (minute, hour and second hands)
Small piece of Balsa wood, same size as clock movement

INSTRUCTIONS

1 We recommend that you take the completed tapestry to a professional framer to be framed, as a circular design is more difficult to block and frame. We do not advise the use of padding behind the canvas in this instance, as the extra thickness can hinder the movement of the clock hands.

2 BEFORE going to the framer, however, a few things need to be done.

The backing board needs to have a 6 mm (1/4 in) hole drilled in the middle of the circle to allow the clock's spindle mechanism to fit through when the hands are assembled.

Also, the centre stitches of the design, which have been left unstitched, must line up with this centre hole in the backing board when it is mounted. Carefully cut the unstitched area ready to later place the spindle through. It is easier to do this before you have the canvas mounted onto the board.

3 When the canvas has been mounted and placed in the frame, clock movements can be attached.

It may be necessary to place a spacer between the backing board and the clock movement mechanism to allow for the secure fastening of the clock hands.

Handy Hint

We suggest you use a piece of Balsa Wood as a spacer. It is very light and easily shaped into the correct size. Make the piece of Balsa the same size as the clock movement, and make sure there is a large enough hole in the centre of it to allow the clock's spindle to fit through.

4 Once the desired fit is obtained, attach the hands to the front of the clock. The hour hand is positioned first, followed by the minute hand. Then place the second hand in position, ensuring all components are firmly locked together.

5 Finally, fit a battery to the clock movement in the space provided, turn it on and adjust the minute and hour hands as required.

Most clock movements have a hanger attached.

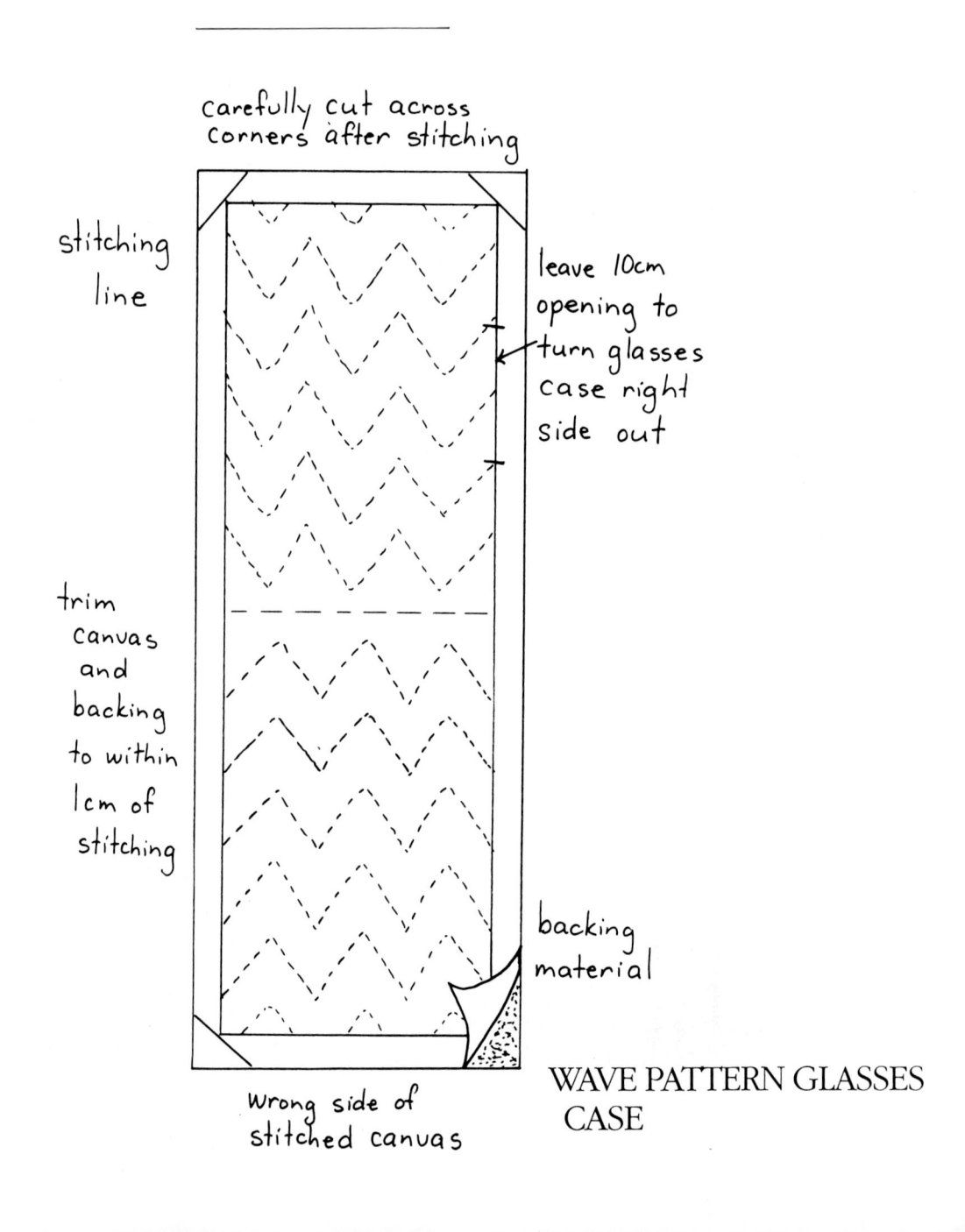

carefully cut across corners after stitching

stitching line

leave 10cm opening to turn glasses case right side out

trim canvas and backing to within 1cm of stitching

backing material

Wrong side of stitched canvas

WAVE PATTERN GLASSES CASE

MAKING UP THE WAVE PATTERN GLASSES CASE

Lining and sewing up the Glasses Case is an easy task, and you will soon have a very stylish and yet practical item to use yourself or give as a gift.

MATERIALS

Small piece of light to medium material for lining
Sewing thread that tones with colours stitched in the tapestry pattern

Invisible nylon thread
Scissors to trim canvas

INSTRUCTIONS

1 Trim the canvas around the design to within 2 cm (1 in) of the stitching.
2 Cut a piece of lining material the same size as the trimmed canvas.
3 Have the lining material right side up and place the stitched canvas wrong side up on top of the lining.
4 Pin the two pieces together, and stitch around all four sides of the design, leaving a 5 cm (2 in) gap along one of the long sides.

5 Trim excess canvas and lining. Carefully cut across each corner to remove excess canvas.
6 Turn the canvas right side out, through the opening left in the side.
7 Press again lightly on the lining side. Fold the lined canvas in half and, using nylon thread, oversew down each long side to form the case. Securely end off the thread.

GLOSSARY

Anchoring Backstitch. A small backstitch used when either beginning or ending off a new thread, to help anchor it after weaving the end into the back of already worked stitches.

Blind Stitch. Small, even topstitching, usually done with 'invisible' nylon thread, which binds two edges of canvas together.

Blocking. The stretching and straightening of a canvas after stitching has been completed but before it is framed or made up into a finished article.

Craft glue. A special glue made especially for use in gluing materials, threads, fabrics, etc. The important thing is that it dries clear and does not spoil the look of the work.

Fibre. Very fine, thread-like segments which are spun together to form threads.

Flexihoop. A two-part hoop which has an outer section that can be adjusted to fit around the material or canvas placed over the inner hoop. The outer hoop can then be tightened to hold the canvas securely.

Floor frame. A special frame, designed to sit on the floor, and onto which the working frame is attached. This leaves both hands free for stitching and is a great time saver. A frame that can be adjusted to suit individual chair positions is the best one to buy, and it makes for many hours of comfortable stitching.

Floss. The name used in the USA for embroidery thread, usually Stranded Cotton.

Interlock canvas. Canvas that has the intersections of the vertical and horizontal threads secured by an extra twist of cotton.

Mass. In references to Candlewicking Knots, means to closely bunch the knots together, working as many as possible into the area to be covered, to give a close, fully textured look.

Medium. The thread, bead, ribbon, etc applied to the canvas in Creative stitching.

Mono. In relation to canvas, means single weave. At the intersection of canvas threads there is only one vertical and one horizontal thread.

Nap. The soft, short hairs or fibres found on the surface of spun threads, especially those spun from natural fibres such as wool and cotton.

Oversew. Small, even stitches sewn over the raw edge of the canvas.

Penelope. The name given to duo or double weave canvas.

Pressing cloth. A specially treated cloth designed to help in the final pressing of fabrics, and used to protect the work from direct contact with the iron.

Re-align. In relation to strands of thread, means to place the strands back together side by side so that they lie next to each other rather than twist around each other.

Stranded. A thread that is made up of a number of individual strands loosely twisted together. When using these types of threads, always strand out the number of strands required and re-align them back together before threading the needle.

Scotchguard. The trade mark for a spray-on chemical treatment designed to protect fabrics, once treated, from stains and soiling. Treated fabric will repel oil, grease and water. Care must be taken not to saturate the canvas.

Tension. The amount of stretch applied to the thread as it is stitched. The tension should be adjusted to achieve the most appropriate coverage of the canvas.

Weave. To work a thread in and out of the canvas or other stitches in a uniform manner.

Working frame. A specially designed, sturdy, rectangular, wooden frame onto which the canvas is sewn before stitching. The frame keeps the canvas taut, making it easier to stitch, and reduces softening of the canvas caused by constant handling.

GUIDE TO SUPPLIERS

The Tapestry Guild Inc
PO Box 102
Baulkham Hills NSW 2153 - Ph (02) 875 1607

The Tapestry Guild has a complete mail order service for Australia and overseas. All supplies mentioned in this book can be purchased from the Guild. Items designed and made specifically for the Guild include fully adjustable floor frames, lap frames, pin cushion bases and hand-made circular wooden frames.

The Tapestry Guild also provides classes, workshops and very comprehensive correspondence courses in Tapestry and Creative Tapestry.

For more information and Mail Order Catalogues, contact the Guild at the above address.

For your nearest stockist of DMC threads, canvas, etc, contact one of the following:

DMC Needlecraft
51-55 Carrington Road
Marrickville NSW 2204 - Ph (02) 559 3088

Dunlicraft
Pullman Road
Wingston
Leicester LE8 2DY UK

DMC Corp USA
Port Kearny
Building 10
South Kearny NJ 07032 USA

Warner Trading Co Ltd
376 Ferry Road
(PO Box 19567)
Christchurch New Zealand

DMC
10 Avenue Led Ru-Rollin
75579 Paris France
CEDEX 12

D.M.C. K.K.
3-7-4-203, Kuramae
Taito-Ku
Tokyo 111 Japan

SATC 43 Somerset Road
(PO Box 3868)
Capetown 8000 RSA

INDEX

Assembling
- Wooden Base Pin Cushion 67
- Tapestry Clock 75,76

Back of canvas 20
Beginning each new thread 18

Canvas
- colour 7
- Interlock Mono 6,23
- Leno 6
- Penelope 7,23
- pre-printed 4,22
- Regular Mono 6

Correct stitching method 16,19
Correcting mistakes 20,21

Design Outlines
- Decor Doorstop 46-47
- Floral Bell Pull 50-51
- Novelty Clowns 54-55

Ending off each thread 19

Floor frame 12
Framing
- professional 65
- in a flexihoop 73

Graphs
- Brick Stitch variation Pin Cushion 44
- Clock 60
- Floral Pin Cushion 44
- Glasses Case 62
- Pink Wave Pattern Pin Cushion 43

Lights 13

Making up
- Decor Doorstop 71,72
- Floral Bell Pull 68-70
- Glasses Case 77

Nap of threads 16

Needle sizes 12
Needle threaders 17

Organising threads 22,42

Scissors 12
Sorting threads 22
Stitch instructions
- Backstitching 38
- Basketweave Stitch 34
- Brick Stitch 35
- Candlewicking Knots 26-27,32
- Canvas Cross Stitch 31
- Continental Stitch 25,29-30
- Double Brick Stitch 35-36
- Double Cross Stitch 26
- Half Cross Stitch 27
- Horizontal Long Stitch 24
- Large Horizontal Brick Stitch 36
- Overstitching 39
- Parisian Stitch 34
- Petit Point Stitch 30
- Split Long Stitch 24
- Tapestry Weaving Stitch 37
- Vertical Long Stitch 24

Tapestry needles 12,17
Threading the needle 17
Thread storage boxes 12
Threads
- length 9-10,16
- Medici Fine Wool 10
- Metallic Ribbon Floss 11
- Pearl 3 Cotton 9
- Pearl 5 Cotton 9
- Ribbon Floss 11
- Soft Embroidery Cotton 8
- Stranded Cotton 10
- Tapestry Wool 7

Transferring the design onto canvas 41-42

Working extra rows 22
Working frames 12,15-16